MW01596115

# THE HIGHEST CALLING OF ALL

## God's Ultimate Purpose For Each Of Us

**An ABLAZE Production by Larry Trammell**

*From the* **"Read And Take Heed!"** *Series*

**Ablaze Publishing**
**P.O. Box 956236**
**Duluth, Georgia 30136**
**(404) 476-0744 or 476-0230**

*Ablaze Publishing is a division of:*
*Ablaze Productions!, Inc.*
*6185 South Buford Highway*
*Suite C-155*
*Norcross, Georgia, 30071*
*U.S.A.*
*(404) 416-0945*

# THE HIGHEST CALLING OF ALL

*God's Ultimate Purpose*
*For Each Of Us*

## An *ABLAZE* Production by *Larry Trammell*

### From the *"Read And Take Heed!"* Series
### ISBN 0-9624370-0-X

**Library of Congress, Catalog Card Number 91-071707**

Scripture quotations marked (NIV) are taken from the HOLY BIBLE, NEW INTERNATIONAL VERSION. Copyright © 1973, 1978, 1984 International Bible Society. Used by permission of Zondervan Bible Publishers.

Scripture quotations marked (AMP), (Amplified), or (Amplified Version) are taken from The Amplified Bible. Old Testament copyright © 1965, 1987 by The Zondervan Corporation. The Amplified New Testament copyright 1958, 1987 by The Lockman Foundation. Used by permission.

Scripture quotations marked (NAS) are taken from the New American Standard Bible, © 1960, 1962, 1963, 1968, 1971, 1972, 1973, 1975, 1977 by The Lockman Foundation. Used by permission.

Scripture quotations marked (NKJV) are taken from the New King James Version. Copyright © 1979, 1980, 1982, Thomas Nelson Inc., Publishers.

Thanks so much to James Strong for his wonderful concordance: "Strong's Exhaustive Concordance of the Bible," published by Riverside Book and Bible House. It is such a blessing, and I have used it very often.

# Dedicated

To you, the reader...
May you be a doer,
and not merely a hearer.
May you walk and possess,
and not merely talk and profess.
May the message of this book
find a place in your heart,
and not just your head.
And may you come to
intimately know the One
to Whom the words herein direct.

# TABLE OF CONTENTS

# A "Five-Fold" Foreword

*"And He gave some as apostles, and some as prophets, and some as evangelists, and some as pastors and teachers..."*
*[Ephesians 4:11; NAS].*

## From an Apostle's Heart:

**THE HIGHEST CALLING OF ALL** is a book that will touch the hearts of those who read it. You will be stirred toward an even more intimate relationship with the Lord and it will fan the flame of any desire you have toward knowing God intimately and in all of His fullness.

It has been my privilege to know Larry Trammell, his precious wife Alice and their children closely over the past several years. Knowing Larry at this level, I have witnessed his prophetic mantel and desire to know God in a real way during the many hours we have spent together. In this book I see Larry pouring forth out of his heart and his communion with the Lord to bless the body of Christ.

The book is full of gems forming a beautiful mosaic and a challenging picture of one moving from the Holy Place into the very Holy of Holies. It shares insights into the preparation and process of coming into that "Highest Calling Of All." Then when we truly know God we are able to reveal Him because we have been in the Holy of Holies with Him!

THE HIGHEST CALLING OF ALL is not a book of 'pat formulas' or 'learned responses' but touches us at the very heart of God and His desire for relationship with us. The book can be lifechanging and make us able ministers of this Gospel through the Holy Spirit to truly reveal God Himself.

Larry, thank you for sharing your heart with the body of Christ. Also, thank you for giving us a chance to re-evaluate how we are doing at "fulfilling the highest calling of all" personally. As one who has been "sent forth," I appreciate it greatly and will certainly recommend it to those we work with and those we are training in preparation for ministry. It will remind us of what truly is *THE HIGHEST CALLING OF ALL!*

**Bill Perry,**
*International Director:*
*Life Schools Of Ministry, Inc. and Frontline Evangelism*
*Phillipines.*

## From a Prophet's Heart:

**My dear brother and faithful prophet,** Larry Trammell, sets forth in these pages an urgent yet intimate call from the Lord of the Church to be in union with Himself, and so fulfill the vision and call of the individual and corporate church in this hour.

**Chris Strong,**
*Our Shepherd's*
*Lithonia, Georgia*

## From An Evangelist's Heart:

**In my nearly three decades as an evangelist,** I have continually been saddened by the spectacle of a Church in chaos and conflict. As I sought God for an explanation of this sordid state of affairs, He revealed to me the underlying reason: His people are pursuing the wrong goals.

For some, of course, the quest is for personal gain, in terms of wealth or recognition. The Bible makes mention of these and the judgment that awaits them. It is not these that break my heart so much as those who have a genuine zeal for God but are amiss in their understanding of Christianity and their relationship with God. They seek holiness, righteousness and the power of God, but fail to realize they received these as a gift of God when they believed in Jesus and were born from above. They strive for what they already possess!

As a result, righteousness and the blessings of God have become objects of competitive quest. Each group or denomination pursues these goals in its own way. Biblical truths, rather than forces for deliverance, become fortresses of defiance. From behind their doctrinal walls, angry, fearful believers fire salvos of contempt against fellow Christians whose convictions fail to conform to their own in every particular. They feverishly defend the traditions of men as though they were the commands of God.

In such an atmosphere, jealousy and selfish ambition abound as conflict and controversy exert their demand for shrewd, resourceful leadership. But, as James 3:16 urgently warns, disorder and every evil thing exist where these attitudes prevail. And can anyone deny the Body of Christ today exhibits the symptoms of this disease, with division, defeat and demonic infiltration rampant in so many congregations and denominations?

If too many Christians are seeking the wrong goals, what should they be pursuing? Larry Trammell presents the answer forcefully but lovingly in this book. As you read it, I hope you will realize how sadly the Church has overlooked the prophetic plea in Hosea 6:6, twice quoted by Jesus:

"For I delight in loyalty rather than sacrifice,
And in knowledge of God rather than burnt offerings."

And that you will join me in praying that this message will have a supernatural impact in helping prepare the Bride for our Savior's return in these last days.

**James Robison,**
*Ft. Worth, Texas*

**From a Pastor's Heart:**

**I met Larry Trammell** in the summer of 1987 when he came to our assembly to help in our praise and worship. As I look back, I know he was from God, but initially, I had my doubts because He said things I had never heard in my circle of friends or other ministries.

He was saying things like, "The Greater Includes The Lesser," and, "Are We Meeting Just To Meet, Or Are We Meeting To Meet Him?" Needless to say, this was new to my way of thinking. However, I have found out that the greater *does* include the lesser...and we are finally attempting *to meet Him first,* and not try to meet each other's needs — which does occur *when* you meet Him.

I have read this book with great excitement in my spirit, and I highly recommend it to every member of the body of Christ.

**David Michael,**
*Faith Cornerstone*
*Atlanta, Georgia*


**From a Teacher's Heart:**

**Many Christians today are seeking** a plan of God without finding joy or contentment as children of God. Some are convinced they must be active in full-time "ministry." In reality they should be seeking God — progressively coming to know Him.

Mr. Trammell's insight into true worship leads believers into a more intimate relationship with the Father.

**Germaine Copeland,**
*Sandy Springs, Georgia*
*Author: Prayers That Avail Much*

The prophet who has a dream,
let him tell a dream;
and he who has My Word,
let him speak My Word faithfully.
What has straw in common
with wheat [for nourishment]?"
says the Lord.
"Is not My Word like fire
[that consumes all that cannot endure the test]?"
says the Lord,
"and like a hammer
that breaks in pieces the rock
[of most stubborn resistance]?"
**Jeremiah 23:28-29;**
**Amplified Version**


"Do not My words do good
to him who walks uprightly?"
**From Micah 2:7;**
**Amplified Version**


"What I tell you in the darkness, speak in the light;
and what you hear whispered in your ear,
proclaim upon the housetops."
**Jesus**
**Matthew 10:27;**
**New American Standard Version**


"Then the Lord put forth His hand and touched my mouth.
And the Lord said to me,
'Behold, I have put My words in your mouth.
See, I have this day appointed you
to the oversight of the nations and of the kingdoms,
to *root out* and *pull down,*
to *destroy* and to *overthrow,*
to *build* and to *plant.*' "
**Jeremiah 1:9-10;**
**Amplified Version**

# Preface
(Don't Skip This!)

**It is with great earnestness and seriousness** that I write this book because, like it or not, and yes, even ready or not, we are all hurtling toward an imminent confrontation with absolute, irrefutable realities. For some it shall be a time of great fulfillment and joy (though certainly not without pain), while for the many it shall be a time of total, overwhelming sorrow and loss. It is my prayer that this book shall be used to help you be ready for "the Day" that is upon us.

In the hustle and bustle of everyday life we can easily lose sight of the fact that our lives are swiftly passing by. Opportunities extended to us today may be lost forever if we do not act upon them — issues of eternal significance may be relegated to matters of seemingly little importance. But Truth stands on its own, regardless of our attitude towards it. Therefore, I urge you to take to heart — leading to positive action — the Truth presented in these pages.

**These are not merely carefully construed writings** concerning Christian doctrine that I have tried to come up with in order to say something that I thought would be nice. No, rather, I have eaten them. They have become a part of my being and everyday experience. And I know that the contents of this book will be life to you if you let them, because they have been life to me!

Some of these words are gentle and easy to take, while some might seem very pointed, even "hard." But do not be afraid of poignant or "hard" words that are born of God — to the lover of Truth, even the seemingly "hard" words from our God are words of comfort and hope because they direct us in paths of righteousness and truly do good to those who walk uprightly.

You will note that the book is divided into sections. Each tends to build upon the foundation laid by the ones preceding it. While I truly desire that readers would read the entire book, I recognize that having sections with a certain "theme" for each one should help those readers who may want to use the book as a type of devotional, as well as benefiting someone who might be looking for some input on a particular topic.

Even though each chapter is written so that it could stand alone (containing a complete message of its own), there is a constant theme and common thread tying them all together — a call for discipleship and a loving relationship with the Living God and His Son, Jesus Christ. We are to grow up in all things into Him, and come to know and express *Him* — not merely things *about* Him.

Let me add here, as well, that you will not find this book to be what for many has become the expected order of spiritually-minded books. This is not a typical "how to," "steps 1-2-3," or a "formula for spiritual growth" treatise.

No, rather, it is a book of inspiring — and for some, probably even inflammatory — Truth; a book that will stir you to examine your heart, judge yourself, and get on with God, if you will but allow its contents to penetrate your heart. Hopefully it will do more than excite you. Instead, my desire is that you be incited and ignited in your quest for God and His wonderful Person and fullness.

As you read this and other writings, be open to looking up any Scripture references that are given if you don't readily recognize them. This will greatly aid in your learning of Scripture, and will serve as a means of verifying the points that are being made. Follow the example of the "noble" Bereans: They received the message of the Kingdom with great eagerness and examined the Scriptures daily to see whether the things Paul presented to them were true. [Acts 17:11].

**In closing this preface,**
I desire to clearly state that I do not claim to "know it all,"

nor do I purport to be better than anyone else. In all honesty, there have been times I've "cussed and fussed" since the words herein were penned, but having found Him Who is the Answer to the enigma of life, I am aware that there is so much more to be known and experienced within Him, and I sincerely ask that you join me in "the Quest."

Thank you, and may the reality of Immanuel be yours always.

**Larry Trammell**

# OUR RELATIONSHIP WITH GOD BEGINS

*"Come to Me, all you who labor and are heavy-laden, and I will give you rest. Take My yoke upon you, and learn of Me..."*
**Jesus**
**[From Matthew 11:28-29; based on Amplified Version]**

*They then said,..."What are we to do to carry out what God requires?" Jesus replied, "This is the work [service] that God asks of you, that you cleave to [**Me**,] the One Whom He has sent."*
**[From John 6:28-29; based on Amplified Version]**

*"You diligently study the Scriptures because you **think** that by them you possess eternal life. These are the Scriptures that testify about Me, yet you refuse to come to Me, so that you may have life."*
**Jesus**
**[John 5:39-40; based on NIV and NAS]**

*"Salvation is found in no one else [other than Jesus Christ of Nazareth], for there is no other name under heaven given to men by which we must be saved."*
**[From Acts 4:12; based on NIV]**

*"I have heard of You by the hearing of the ear, but now my eye sees You. Therefore I abhor myself, and repent in dust and ashes."*
**[Job 42:5-6; NKJV]**

# 1.

# The Highest Calling Of All
## *Or*
## First Things First

**The highest calling of all!**

Have you ever given it any thought? Have you ever wondered what is the greatest, best, and most special thing that one could do to really please the Lord? What is *the ultimate calling* that God places on individuals?

If one were to ask God's people what they thought was the highest calling of all, many would think of some so called "full-time" ministry vocation, perhaps like being a pastor or other "staff member" with a Christian fellowship.

Still others would imagine a ministry of great works of power done in the name of Jesus as a means of reaching the world. To these people, raising the dead, healing the sick, casting out demons and so forth would surely be the highest calling of all.

Then again, others would say it would be to preach the Gospel of Jesus Christ to the lost all over the world, seeing multitudes come to the Savior and set free from their prison of self and sin.

And, of course, many would think that intercessory prayer and such — effectual but "hidden" ministries — must surely constitute the highest calling of all.

Nevertheless, as precious and valuable as each of these things are when born of God, they are not the highest calling of all.

Also, the highest calling of all is not some unique, "once-in-a-hundred-years-super-type-ministry" that is extended only to a small, elite, unique corps of the body of Christ — some kind of "chosen of the chosen," so to speak. No, on the contrary, the highest calling of all is given to every man, woman, boy, and girl on the face of the earth!

## No exclusiveness here!

The call is to *everyone,* regardless of background, status, education or the lack thereof, vocation, or occupation. Whether we be an apostle, posthole digger, or both, the highest calling of all is extended to each one of us.

## "Then what is it?" you may ask.

The highest calling of all is simply and profoundly this: to intimately know the True and Living God and He Whom He has sent — Jesus Christ, and then, as a result of this established relationship with the Lord, to "let God arise" [Psalm 68:1], allowing Him to reveal Himself through us to His creation and call it back to Himself.

In short, *the highest calling of all is to know God and then to reveal God!*

Even so, many people have become disillusioned and frustrated with their lives because they feel that their occupations and day to day activities are of little or no importance, especially in light of what they think are special and valuable callings in God's kingdom:

"Why am I just a housewife, (businessman, teacher, carpenter, or what have you)," they reason, "when I could be doing something that's really important, like being a missionary, or a pastor, or fulfilling my calling to be a prophet, or whatever? I must be just wasting my life!"

## No!

This persuasion certainly does not come from the Lord of Glory who calls them.

On the contrary, if God has called us to any task, regardless of how menial and unimportant it might seem in the eyes of others, there is nothing higher that we can do.

"But if I was just involved in a 'full-time ministry!' " one might say.

What???

Isn't all of our time and all of our life the Lord's? Is He not Lord over *every* facet of our beings?

## *All* believers are in full-time ministry.

If someone is truly a child of God, regardless of their station or lot in life, they *are* in full-time ministry — from the moment they were born of God!

Truly, change may be ahead for us, and more blatant expressions of our faith in the Lord, but we must realize that every moment of our life, not just some special time off in the future, is precious and special to the Lord. Right where we are we can be a tool in the hand of the Lord, used to touch others and war against satanic forces, if we would but offer ourselves unreservedly to the Lord and follow the leadings of His Spirit in all things.

"But if I could just be doing something 'spiritual,' " someone might add.

We must realize spirituality is doing the will of the Lord, regardless of what it is. If God calls someone to be a farmer, or whatever else, there is *nothing* they can do more spiritual.

## Obedience to God *is* spirituality.

If any of us attempted to be a pastor because we thought it was more spiritual, when God would have us to be a deliveryman, technician, or anything else, our pastoring would grieve the Holy Spirit and disappoint our Father.

Remember, too, that timing is very important. Even if we are called to eventually be doing something else, if God has us doing something other than our final destiny for a while, even a great while, we must see to it that we keep our eyes on Him and not on our concepts of what we think we should be doing.

## We are to bloom where we are planted.

Remember: Father knows best! Be encouraged, knowing that in every person's life there is a time of preparation.

Moses was eighty years old when he was sent forth by God. It was years before Paul embarked on his first missionary journey after meeting the Lord Jesus. And yes, even Jesus our Lord was a carpenter, a businessman, until He was thirty years old! In each of these examples, and in so many others listed in Scripture, we see a servant of God, eventually mightily used by Him, going through a God-ordained period of preparation.

An interesting and thrilling side-thought that goes along with this is that if we are being prepared for a future work, the hearts of those to whom we will one day minister are surely being prepared to receive what we have from God.

So we mustn't get anxious.

We must not get ahead of the Lord.

## No More "Sacred" Or "Secular":

Furthermore, for a committed disciple of Jesus Christ, in one sense the terms "sacred" and "secular" begin to disappear from his experience; not that there is a denial of the existence of good and evil, or light and darkness, but simply because his whole life becomes a sacrament, sacred and dedicated to the Lord, no matter what he might be doing. He doesn't look for a so called "sacred" enterprise or duty, neither does he scorn or regard as of lesser importance that which others term as "secular." His only concern is to know and please God his Father. Therefore, he does not acknowledge "sacred" or "secular" for his own life, but only the Lord Himself.

As a matter of fact, the majority of the most dramatic leadings and words from God that I've received came when I was not even consciously expecting them. I was simply going about my day to day, "secular" activities, so to speak.

One of these occurred sometime in 1975. I was working as a train-brake mechanic in a noisy, dirty, hot repair shop. On this particular day, I was testing air brakes that had been repaired. It required concentration, so I was paying close attention to what I was doing. I am emphasizing these details because I want to make clear that I was not in any kind of "conscious" communion with the Lord. I wasn't focusing on praying. I wasn't singing psalms. I was simply working at my job.

## Suddenly, the Lord spoke to me.

Not audibly, but so very clearly through my spirit to my mind, He spoke. It was totally unexpected.

After all, the work environment and the demands of my responsibilities were not exactly conducive to what most would consider an atmosphere of prayer and communion with the Lord. Yet, the Lord spoke, and this is what He said:

## "Pray for Hartwell. It's on fire."

Now my wife ("Alice") and I had at the time a house at Lake Hartwell, Georgia. We referred to this house as "Hartwell," so the Lord did the same. It was a little tinderbox, easily combustible, because of its age and materials. Some tenants were presently renting the place. Believe me, I wasn't thinking about Hartwell at all when the Lord spoke to me.

Immediately, I went up to several Christian brothers that were working there also. I told them what the Lord had said and requested that they pray. I then went back to my test rack and did something similar to what Ezekiel the prophet did when he prophesied to certain mountains [Ezekiel 35:1-2; 36:1] — I spoke directly to the fire.

I said, "Fire, I come against you in the name of Jesus and I put you out!"

That's it. Nothing fancy.

## No long, elaborate prayer.

No getting down on my knees, washing the grease off of my hands, putting on clean clothes, or even leaving my workstation.

I simply did what the Lord told me to do, then I forgot about it and continued testing the brakes.

When I arrived home that evening, one of the first

things Alice said was, "You'll never guess what happened today."

"Hartwell caught on fire," I said.

"How did you know???" she asked, completely surprised; her eyes wide with wonder and amazement...

Man, did I rejoice! Not because my house caught on fire, but because I saw that I had truly heard and recognized His voice.

After I had calmed down from shouting and leaping and praising God, Alice explained what happened. "The folks that are renting Hartwell called and said that an electrical fire broke out in the walls where they couldn't get to it, and the fire 'mysteriously went out by itself.' "

**Ha-ha.** *Sure* **— by itself!**

Looking back at this experience, I see clearly that there was nothing "religious" about it, in the usual sense of the word...

No liturgy.

No peaceful surroundings.

Not even any conscious focus on the Lord until He spoke. To the contrary, I was very much engrossed in my work and duties.

**Yet this is so often how the Lord works.**

He loves to see the menial elevated to importance by our response to His Presence and His will.

He desires to lift the temporal into the eternal.

He desires to flood us with Himself and find us sensitive to Him at all times, whether we are consciously thinking about Him or not.

On call twenty-four hours a day. Seven days a week. Servants of the Most High God, ready and willing to do His bidding.

**Remember:**

Yieldedness to God is a condition of the heart and an attitude of the mind. We can be totally submitted and open to God while engaging in the events of everyday life.

This is not denying the value and need of having specified times to seek His face. However, we don't have to be consciously aware of the Lord to be in tune with Him. We don't always have to be in a certain position or situation to hear Him speak.

**If we are sensitive and willing,**

He can communicate to us whenever He chooses to do so.

Finally, we need not be concerned with missing God's best and settling for something less if we will but simply get first things first...

First, we must secure and maintain an intimate relationship and fellowship with the Lord, being faithful to Him and not to any pre-conceived idea that may come to us. We must stay vitally and constantly in tune with the Spirit of God, always abiding in union with the Lord Jesus by listening to Him and obeying Him.

Then, we will never go wrong, and all our ways will be pleasing to Him because we will be constantly walking in His will, delighting His heart.

If we will press on to know the Lord and allow Him total access to us at all times — available to Him, at His disposal, each and every moment of every day, then He will not be limited to only revealing Himself *to us*. He will then also be able to "arise" and reveal Himself *in us* and *through us,* in *His* way and at *His* direction.

**Remember the highest calling of all:**

*To know God and then, in union with the Holy Spirit, to reveal God!*

2.

# The Journey

**The storm had pounded the traveler unrelentingly for days.** Without mercy, the biting wind howled and hissed, whipping him in the face as torrential rains pounded away at his will to struggle onward. Sitting in the mud, he wondered if the thick, swirling sea of black clouds would mock the day and hide the sun forever.

Throughout the long journey, dangerous traps and threatening situations had seemed to be a constant challenge. Some inflicted pain. Still others seductively appealed to him in an effort to keep him from attaining his goal...

Many times he had encountered hardened murderers, thieves, and liars — cunning and cruel — poised and eager to kill, steal, and destroy.

And just off the path were tantalizing trees laden with alluring fruit. But he had seen how all who had even just a taste of it were left more hungry and empty than before.

**"I'm so tired," the pilgrim said to himself.**

"This journey is more than I imagined. The road is so steep that I can hardly press forward. And it's so narrow! I bet those who make their homes alongside the road aren't attacked nearly as much as I am.

"I'm freezing and I haven't seen the sun for so long. How can I be expected to walk in its light like I was told when I can't see it or even feel it? I saw the way to go before this storm began, but now the path is so dark that I can hardly see a thing. It's just not fair for me to have such hard times. And so many told me that it was going to be easy!!! It's just not worth the pain and trouble anymore..."

**And so, he gave up his pilgrimage.**

Alas! He settled for a dusty plot beside the path rather than completing his intended course, thereby gaining the fullness of his inheritance as a child and heir of the Great King! The riches and authority that awaited him would have benefited many others as well as himself.

*Tragically, throughout history, most of the Church has done the same thing.*

Probably every disciple of Jesus Christ can relate to our weary and beguiled pilgrim and his difficult quest. Haven't we all felt discouraged at times, feeling as though we would never be able or perhaps even willing to fulfill God's call and desire for us?

I know I have.

All of us deal with forces and circumstances that blast us with such fierceness and intensity that it feels as if all Hell has been unleashed against us. And you know, that is quite an accurate way to put it...

The Scriptures reveal that we have a determined, crafty, and invisible enemy who is at war with us (whether we recognize it or even believe it or not!) — Satan and his vast and dedicated army of demons. They delight to inflict pain and are bent on our destruction. Furthermore, they expend a great deal of effort attempting to impede the progress of anyone determined to follow the True and Living Lord — Jesus Christ.

## Temptations

(represented by the fruit trees beside the path), often seem innocent, even beneficial, to us. However, they distract and detract travelers from their pursuit of the King and His heavenly kingdom. They only lead to disillusionment, misdirection, and wasted time at best. At worst, these diversions may cause us to give up our spiritual trek altogether...

The Church has been issued a glorious command from the God of Glory to pursue Him and His kingdom. Unfortunately, having gotten our focus off of Jesus, most of us have become disillusioned and our hearts have grown hardened. The result is a settling for something other than what the Lord God intends.

Furthermore, not only have we settled for less, we have tried to convince ourselves that it is the Lord's best. Calling brass "gold," and mistaking frenzied activity as a proof of life, we have deceived ourselves and rendered ourselves largely ineffective in bringing change to this world so full of rebellion and need.

## But such is the fruit of compromise.

Many of us have made ourselves at home in this pagan world instead of being "strangers and pilgrims" passing through. [See Hebrews 11:13; 13:13-14; 1 Peter 1:1, 17; 2:11].

Thus, multitudes suffer needlessly. For in not completing our journey, we forfeit victory for ourselves as well as others.

*However, the Church's story is still in the process of being written.* Each one who is a part of the body of Christ has a critical role in the way this story will end.

## The Spirit of God is calling with clarity, urgency,

and frequency to those who by their willingness to obey Him have "ears to hear." He is saying that the Church's finest hour is upon us! The greatest day in the history of the Church is dawning!

Who will answer His call to be a part of God's final great move at the end of this present age???

God is even now equipping those who are willing and obedient to complete the journey with overwhelming victory, even though it be through tremendous resistance from a frightened and desperate enemy. We need not be "burned out," worn to a frazzle due to our trying to accomplish God's will without Him, or by futilely trying to impress Him with our own works.

No, instead, as we regain our first love, pursuing the Lord for Who He is, and not become enamored with this present life, we shall experience a walk of power and purity that we've only possibly heard of or dreamed about.

There is an answer for those ready to settle for less than God's best! There is a call that is coming forth with greater and greater intensity! There is a fresh anointing that awaits to refresh and empower those who pursue *Him* Who anoints!

We must gather together around "Shiloh" [See Genesis 49:10; NKJV] — "the Lord Jesus." He, our present and eternal Reward, shall enable us to endure and overcome, completing our course in faith, and thus gain a glorious, unashamed entrance into His kingdom with great, unending joy!

The Day of the Lord — a day of challenge, preparation, battle, and victory is upon us. Will we pursue the Goal with vigor? Will we, out of our love for the Lord Jesus, fulfill God's highest calling?

## Let us rouse ourselves and get on with the journey!

It is true that we shall encounter many perils and tests along the way. However, we shall discover that our glorious journey contains joy that is unspeakable, victory that is secured, and an ultimate Goal and Reward beyond comprehension—even the Lord God Himself! [See Genesis 15:1; NKJV].

## Now just as a great, structurally sound house

must have a firm foundation, every person's life must be built on pure, firm, basic yet critically important Truth. *A foundation can remain without a building, but a building cannot remain without a foundation.* Therefore, in the remaining nine chapters of this first section, let's get "back to basics," making sure that we are on a good footing and firm foundation. In later sections, we shall explore what some would call "deeper" aspects of the Truth, but what we study in the next few pages is no less important. Indeed, to the contrary, the following "basics" are indispensable prerequisites that we must personally experience before we can apprehend further things:

*First* a foundation, *then* a building...

So, regardless of our present spiritual state of being, whether we be mature in Christ or a babe in Christ, a seasoned saint or even a searching skeptic, let's now begin to consider the qualifications and preparations required of those who desire to both begin *and* complete "The Journey..."

# 3.

# Back To Basics *or* FIRST Relationship With God, THEN Fellowship With God

**Before we can enjoy the fullness** of fellowship with God, we must first have an established relationship with Him. We must be born into His family, becoming one of His children. Scripture is clear in pointing out that just because God is the Creator of all, He is not the Father of all. [John 8:44].

When Jesus spoke of being born again [John 3:5-7; 6:63], He was speaking of a spiritual rebirth. Our willful rebellion against God has caused us to become dead towards Him. We have been cut off from relationship and intimacy with Him.

Therefore, we all would remain separated from God forever without a sovereign work of His "grace," which is "His undeserved power and favor." As a matter of fact, without such a work on His part, we wouldn't even *desire* a relationship with Him! For Jesus Himself revealed that no man can come to Him unless the Father draws him. [John 6:65]. So if we have any inclination towards a genuine relationship with the Living God, it is totally because the Lord is wooing us to Himself.

Furthermore, merely purposing to do good deeds and "staying out of trouble" will not secure a relationship with God. It is not accomplished by joining some philanthropic organization, or by going to what a number of people call "church." I say that they *call* it "church" because in actuality the Church is made up of the true people of God, not the building in which they meet, nor some denomination or other organization that they may join. In short, the Church is an *organism* made-up of many members, not an *organization* made-up of many members.

True *Christ*ianity is not the *church*ianity that most of the world has seen. Therefore,

## "playing church" won't save anyone.

Relationship with God is not secured by just "cleaning-up our act" or getting our name on a membership roll.

On the other hand, neither is relationship and fellowship with God accomplished by some "easy believism" which is not true believing in the biblical sense of the word. Someone may teach a parrot to quote Scriptures, claim promises, and say all sorts of "right things," but that would not mean that the parrot was saved! For you see, salvation hinges on more than merely saying or believing the right things, or acknowledging that something is true.

## For example, remember that even the demons believe some correct doctrine.

A number of them were willing to admit Who Jesus is and were even willing to confess Him in front of others. [See Matthew 8:29; Mark 1:24; 5:7; Luke 8:28]. Nevertheless, the demons are not saved. They are damned, though they have a knowledge of the Truth, because they have hardened their hearts, refusing to embrace the Truth. They do not willingly submit to Jesus as Lord.

Their heads are full of knowledge, but their hearts are full of darkness.

Like these demons, many people walk through life with much head knowledge, but not knowledge of the heart! That is, they know many facts about the Kingdom and its Lord, but they do not choose to submit to His lordship and come to *really* **know** Him.

Our profession lacks possession if we have not truly turned from our selfish desires to pursue the Lord and His desires.

*Bended **knees** do not necessarily indicate a bended **heart!***

Remember what the Lord Jesus said, "Not everyone who says to me 'Lord, Lord,' will enter the kingdom of Heaven, but only He who does the will of My Father Who is in Heaven." [Matthew 7:21; based on NIV].

So what is required of us to enter into relationship with the Lord? We must repent and believe on the Lord Jesus Christ.

"Repent" means "to change our minds; to turn from one direction and pursuit to go a different way."

"Believe on the Lord Jesus Christ" means "to cling to and totally rely on the Lord Jesus Himself, willingly submitting to Him as our only Lord in all things." True believing that leads to salvation requires us to know and love the Lord Jesus Himself, and not just things about Him.

Therefore, "to repent and believe on the Lord Jesus Christ" means "to turn from our own pursuits, selfish ambitions, lusts, loves, and concepts, to pursue the Lord Jesus Christ, totally and unreservedly." We are to live to please *Him* (not ourselves) and fulfill His will.

## Salvation is more than "fire insurance."

Salvation is more than just being saved *from* something. It also and primarily refers to being saved *for* something!

You see, many people, when they think of salvation, imagine it to be mainly a "saving *from* Hell that we might "go *to* Heaven." But these are just wonderful by-products of God's ultimate intent in saving sinners, which is to establish and develop a relationship with them, revealing Himself to them, then in them, then through them.

His plan is to save us, both *from* sin and Hell, and *for* His eternal purposes.

Also, when the Scriptures refer to eternal life, they are not merely speaking of living forever. While it is true that the people of God will enjoy ceaseless existence, this is not the central focus of eternal life.

**Furthermore, eternal life is not readily experienced by every child of God!**

Consider 1 Timothy 6:12. Here Paul encourages Timothy — a devout and steadfast believer in the Lord Jesus Christ, and a leader in the Church — to lay hold of the eternal life to which he had been summoned. If eternal life was something automatically experienced in fullness by being one of God's children, Paul would not have counseled Timothy to lay hold of it, for Timothy was certainly a child of God.

## So what is eternal life?

It is intimate, ongoing relationship and fellowship with the only true God and His Son — Jesus Christ. Our Lord Jesus Himself said, "And this is eternal life: [it means] to know (to perceive, recognize, become acquainted with and understand) You, the only true and real God, and [likewise] to know Him, Jesus [as the] Christ, the Anointed One, the Messiah, Whom You have sent." [John 17:3; Amplified Version].

This is why Paul instructed Timothy to lay hold of it. Paul knew that just because Timothy belonged to God did not necessarily mean that he was growing more deeply acquainted with the Lord, coming to more intimately know the Lord Himself, and not just things about Him.

Also, salvation is not just something the Lord gives us apart from Himself...

## *He* is salvation!

Consider the name of the Son of God — "Jesus." His name is a transliteration of the Hebrew "Joshua," meaning "Jehovah is salvation." [From Vine's Expository Dictionary]. Psalm 27:1; 38:22; 62:2, 6; 118:14; and Isaiah 12:2 are Scriptures that refer to God Himself being salvation.

So we see that salvation and eternal life are not just things that the Lord gives us apart from Himself. They are a part of His Person and the intimate union and fellowship with Him to which He is calling us! All of God's blessings and gifts to us are in His Son, and they are received and experienced only to the degree that we know *Him!*

The Lord, desiring to begin this work of revealing Himself to us, "paves the way," so to speak, by first revealing ourselves and our great need to us. He accomplishes this by applying His commands and ways of proper living to our hearts, showing us how far we have gone "off-target;" how far we've "missed the mark." That is the reason the Law of God in the Old Testament, and not just the words of the New, are so vital to us, because without the Law we would not even have a knowledge of what sin is. [Romans 7:7].

When the Law is applied to our hearts, we see, not just hear, that we are rebellious anarchists against the Lord God. We learn of His holiness and our lack thereof. We see that truly we are sinners who deserve death and utter damnation, and who desperately need a Savior.

**Yes, the Law of God has a vital part in leading us to Christ.**

It is true that having a knowledge of the Law and a sincere and earnest attempt to fulfill it cannot save us, but as we've seen, God uses the Law to prepare us to receive Jesus, the Savior. He is our only and sure hope of escaping the Law's demands for justice. Furthermore, He alone can enable us to fulfill the demands of the Law of total conformity to God's will and ways.

So, due to the application of the Law to our heart and mind by the Holy Spirit, we see our desperate plight of being bound by sin ("sin" is "disobedience against the Law of God; all rebellion against Him") and heading for Hell. We are shown that we are without God, and, therefore, without hope [Ephesians 2:12b]. This produces brokenness and recognition of utter need before the Lord.

The Holy Spirit then strives with us to cast ourselves unreservedly on the Lord's mercies. We must submit to Jesus the Christ as our only Lord and acknowledge that

He is the One sent from God Who died in our place for our rebellion. Furthermore, the Holy Spirit reveals that Jesus was also raised from the dead by God, having fully paid the penalty for sin.

## If we see and embrace these things,

turning from our old lives of independence from God so that we can lay hold of the Lord Jesus to be our very Life, the Spirit of God will cause us to be "born from above." That is, we will be "reborn spiritually" and will then be able to perceive and pursue the Kingdom of God. For unless we are born again in our spirit, we cannot see or experience the Kingdom of God. [John 3:3].

This rebirth experience involves the forgiveness of our sins, the cleansing of our spirit, and the actual joining together of our spirit with the Spirit of the Lord. Then, as we choose to follow the inclinations of the new life within us (*His* very life), right and proper living according to God's standards will be produced.

## Let us give ourselves completely to Jesus.

He has paid the price to buy us back from the "slave block" of selfishness, sin, and death. If we are hearing His voice, we must not harden our hearts, but instead call out to Him, turning to Him and believing on Him. For it is only by coming to Him, needy and receptive, that we can ever please God and be at peace with Him and ourselves.

It's our move...

If we first establish relationship with Him, the way will be opened for us to enjoy wonderful, intimate fellowship with Him, beyond what we can even imagine!

## 4.

# Away With Religious Forms And Concepts! *or* Purely Form Or Formed Purely?

**More will probably be damned** because of false security engendered by religion than all the other vices of the world combined! By "religion" we are meaning, in this instance, "the adherence to rituals, observances, and such, supposing that to do so one can secure favor with God and enjoy a relationship with Him."

However, just as it is possible to know about a country's leaders without ever having met or seen them, and just as it is possible to know the language of a country without going there, it is possible to know facts about the Living God and His kingdom without knowing Him personally or being one of His people. Knowledge *about* God and His kingdom can never substitute for the knowledge *of* God and His kingdom.

### Substitutes leave us destitute.

Away with religious forms and concepts that substitute for a genuine relationship with the Living God!

Away with religious and social pretenses that damn souls by deluding them to base their eternal hope on ritual and empty form instead of on the only source of present and eternal hope and comfort — the Lord God Himself!

Lip service and an outward show of commitment to God are no substitutes for an inward change of heart that causes us to cling to Him and always obediently follow the leadings of His Spirit.

We must recognize our utter helplessness and need for the Lord, turn from the lures and empty promises of this world system (including the religious formulas and rituals of men), and unreservedly cast ourselves on the mercies of the Lord. Thus we will allow Him to form us, as a potter does the clay, into vessels of His own making and after His pleasure.

Nothing can substitute for a genuine and ongoing relationship with the Living God, *especially a religious substitute.*

Recall Jesus' denunciation of scribes and pharisees in Matthew 23 for traveling over land and sea to make one convert, and afterwards making him twice as much a child of Hell than they.

### Amazing!

Here the Lord Jesus is showing that it would have been better to have left this "convert" in his heathenism and worldly bondage than to introduce him to the truth in a distorted manner and perception, snaring him in a religious bondage!

These leaders, having in the Law the embodiment of knowledge and truth [Romans 2:20], would go to great lengths to indoctrinate the heathen. But, since these leaders only had a "head knowledge" of the truth, and had not allowed it to penetrate and renew their hardened hearts, they developed converts who, like them, had a form of godliness but denied its power. [And what is "the power of godliness?" It is "God Himself, revealing His character and attributes to, in, and through those who establish and maintain a relationship with Him."]. Jesus was describing and denouncing a classic case of the blind leading the blind, with both of them falling into a ditch. [Matthew 15:14].

### How tragic it is

to know that multitudes have settled for an empty though often lavish system of rituals, codes, rules, forms, and formulas as a substitute for a vibrant, personal, ongoing relationship with the Father and His Son by the Holy Spirit!

**Many, claiming to know God,**

have been presented a portion of the truth by those who do not know Him Who is the Truth, and have been deluded. Having changed some of their ways and having begun to follow a new, so called "Christian" system of religious works and observances, they presume that they have entered a safe "harbor" for their souls.

Unfortunately, they don't realize that they're worse off now than they were before! At least, before, they were *honestly* without hope — lost — in the world. Now, due to wrong teaching and persuasion, these so called "converts" are claiming deliverance when they have not met the Deliverer; salvation when they've not met the Savior! They've been sold a subtle, damning lie.

*There is NO substitute for genuine, intimate relationship with the Living God!*

5.

# Do We Know The Scriptures *And* The Word Of God?

**Picture someone about to embark on a journey** to the destination of their dreams. With great anticipation and zeal they get out and study a map which clearly shows them where they are and the path to take to reach their goal. How foolish we would think that person to be if they thought that to see the destination on the map would be the same as literally getting there!

Nevertheless, in a similar fashion, there are many who, desirous to know Jesus and the things of His kingdom, will study the Scriptures with great commitment and eagerness, only to wrongly conclude that because they know *about* Jesus they really know *Him*.

There is a tremendous amount of difference.

Recall John 5:39 and 40, where Jesus told some devoutly religious folks, "You search the Scriptures for in them you *think* you have eternal life; and these are they that testify about Me, but you refuse to come to *Me* that you might have life."

Here Jesus validates the Scriptures as He always did, stating that they do testify about Him. However, He clearly shows at the same time that the Scriptures are not an end in themselves.

**Rather, *He* is the end. *He* is the destination.**

The intimate, personal, ongoing knowledge of Him is the goal of existence!

The Jewish leaders of Jesus' day were astute scholars of all the Scriptures that existed in their time, spending an

enormous amount of their time absorbing the message of
the letter of the Scriptures. Yet that is where their perception ended, and though they could quote much Scripture
from memory, when the Word of God was made flesh and
came among them, they crucified Him.

## They knew the Scriptures, but they did not know the Word of God!

They did not mix their study of Scripture with "faith" —
"the perception and pursuit of the Kingdom of God."

Therefore, they did not cultivate and maintain an absolute and helpless reliance on the Lord. Instead, they became full of pride, thinking themselves sufficient before
God because they knew and applied their interpretations
of the Scriptures. Not realizing God's intent to use the
Scriptures to spur them on to seek God Himself, these
folks settled for a knowledge *about* God instead of pressing
on to know Him personally.

As a result, they developed a form of godliness but denied the power of it. [See 2 Timothy 3:5]. That is, they
knew concepts, neat phrases, and good doctrine, but they
settled for this knowledge, refusing to know Him Who is
the Power of Godliness.

They had allowed the good to become the enemy of the
best, not realizing that the greater includes the lesser.

## The Scriptures do not interpret God.

No, God must interpret the Scriptures! [See 2 Peter
1:20-21].

Remember, knowledge alone puffs us up, which cuts us
off from God's grace. "God resists the proud, but gives
grace to the humble" — those teachable and knowing their
need of more than what they have. [James 4:6; 1 Peter 5:5.
Also see 1 Corinthians 8:1; James 4:6; Proverbs 3:34;
Galatians 5:4].

## Don't settle for gifts and miss the Giver!

The Scriptures, though divinely given, are not an end in
themselves. Jesus is! *He* is the Ultimate, the Goal, the

Way, the Truth, the Life, the Quest, our All in all.

The Spirit of God does indeed utilize the Scriptures to lead us to the Person of Jesus Christ, much like a map shows us the way or a compass points us in the direction of our goal. And as we continue to seek the Lord, following the instructions and directions of our "map and compass," we are brought more and more into the knowledge of and intimate relationship with the Living God and He Whom He has sent — Jesus Christ.

You see, the need is for relationship *with* God, not just knowledge *about* God. Indeed, all of God's dealings and methods with us are intended to bring us to a greater awareness of, hunger for, and union with Himself. This intimacy is what God is after; not a distant acquaintance with high-minded, learned people who know about Him but don't really know Him.

**The Scriptures can kill or give life.**

Yes, apart from a vital contact with the Living God, the Scriptures can kill. The "letter," that is, the words of the Scriptures alone, kills. Only the Spirit gives life. [2 Corinthians 3:6].

Remember that a divinely inspired, leather-bound Book is not on the Throne of Glory. The Person Who is called "The Word of God" [See Revelation 19:13] — the Lord Jesus Christ — is sitting upon that throne!

It is true that we find instruction, solace, yes, thorough equipping through the Scriptures as they are used by the Spirit of God in our lives. [2 Timothy 3:16-17]. However, let us not settle for just a knowledge of the Scriptures, neglecting to intimately know the One to Whom the Scriptures lead: Jesus Christ — He Who is the Word of God!

*Do **We** Know The Scriptures **And** The Word of God?*

# 6.

# Lord, Lord!

**Mere lip service is not enough;** loudly *professing* faith without *possessing* it will not do. The eternal kingdom of the Lord Jesus does not await those who only cry "Lord, Lord," as they flock to Him. They also must obey what He says, which always conforms to His Father's will.

Many speak loudly of Jesus before men to be seen by them while denying Him and bringing reproach to His name by not living according to His standards. Whoever claims to know God, but does not obey Him, is a liar, and the Truth is not in him. [See 1 John 2:4].

Jesus said, "Why do you call Me 'Lord, Lord,' and do not do what I say?" [Luke 6:46; NIV]. On the great day of God's Judgment, when He will judge everyone according to the things they have done [Revelation 20:11-15], many will cry out for mercy, reminding Jesus of their speaking to others in His behalf, having victory over satanic forces by His power, and doing other mighty deeds while claiming to be His representatives. Nevertheless, those who did not relinquish their selfish pursuits for *His* interests, those who did not truly desire closeness with Him, He will cast from His presence, reminding them of their hypocrisy and lack of genuine relationship with Him. [Matthew 7:21-23].

**Hear as He speaks to those who would follow Him:**

"I have loved you just as My Father has loved Me, but you must make a continual choice to abide in My love by obeying Me. Only those who follow My leading, obeying My voice, are My friends, and only those who choose to seek out and obey the leadings of God's Holy Spirit will know the joys and fulfillment of being known as God's children.

"Do not take My mercy extended to you lightly. If it was not for My choosing you, you never would have come to Me, for in and of yourself you would have no inclination towards the Truth.

"Furthermore, I have not called you without a purpose. You are to be a living testimony before others concerning Me and My kingdom, not only with words, but with a consistent life of good deeds. This kind of life will spring only from a sincere and seeking heart — not one self-sufficient and full of guile and pride.

"You are like a branch that must stay attached to the Vine — Me — in order to bring forth life. You will undergo cleansing by God's Word, and it will sometimes be painful, seemingly cutting back what you have to offer. However, know that My Father, like a wise and caring gardener, is merely 'pruning' you, so to speak. He desires to make you better suited to bring forth even more life and more excellent fruit.

"Also, His pruning is infinitely more to be desired than His rejection due to someone's lack of response and resistance to His dealings! So choose to respond positively to My Father's dealings, and follow Me in word and deed, which are the natural results of a life taken-up and in love with Me.

**"However, don't substitute works for relationship.** The vital issue is as it has always been: Not so much what you've done in My name, but rather, do you know Me intimately?

"Are you getting to know Me better? Do you thrive on a union with Me that is producing good works as a matter of course, or do you think that because you do things, even *good* things, in an attempt to testify in My behalf, that such efforts are pleasing to Me apart from vital union with Me?

**"Do not be deceived concerning this.**

"Your works do not produce good standing with Me, but

should flow out of an established, growing relationship that We have and enjoy. Remember: Works do not produce relationship with Me, but relationship with Me will produce works!

"Knowing that Our relationship is a gift of God, and not something that you can ever earn, prevents you from being able to boast that you deserve God's notice or mercy. For all deserve death, but God is merciful."

**Let us therefore examine ourselves,**

making certain that we are abiding in the faith. And let us keep our hearts set continually on pleasing the Lord, pursuing His kingdom, always choosing the way of obedience, and coming to really know the Lord in an intimate, personal way.

We must be doers of God's word, will, and way, and not hearers only, deceiving ourselves. [James 1:22-25].

Remember: "The one that obeys Me is the one that truly loves Me." [John 14:21]. Saying "Lord, Lord," to Jesus will only add to our condemnation if we do not *do* what He says!!

## Lord, Lord! (a song)

*Not everyone that says to Jesus,*
*"Lord, Lord,"*
*will enter into the Kingdom —*
*but he who does His Father's will.*
*"For many there be that proclaim*
*My name in these days in men's hearing,*
*but they deny Me*
*by the lives they live.*

*(Chorus): "Why, why call Me Lord and*
*not do what I say?*
*Many will stand before Me*
*on that Great Day and say,*
*'Lord, Lord!*

*We prophesied in Your name,*
*cast out demons in Your name,*
*did many mighty works in Your name...'*
*and then they'll hear Me say,*
*Depart from Me, you that do iniquity.*
*I never knew you."*

*"As the Father has loved me,*
*so have I loved you,*
*if you obey My commands*
*you'll remain within My love (**if** you obey).*
*"You are My friends*
*if you do what I command,*
*and will be God's sons*
*if by His Spirit you're led.*
*"For you've not chosen Me,*
*but I've chosen you*
*that you might go forth*
*and bear much fruit (**much** fruit).*
*"For every fruitful branch in Me*
*My Father cleans by pruning,*
*but every worthless branch He cuts away!"*

*(Chorus): "Why, why call Me Lord and*
*not do what I say?*
*Many will stand before Me*
*on that Great Day and say,*
*'Lord, Lord!*
*We prophesied in Your name,*
*cast out demons in Your name (please Lord!)*
*we've done many mighty works in Your name...'*
*and then they'll hear Me say,*
*Depart from Me, you that do iniquity.*
*I never knew you."*

*I want to know You!*

*Does He know me and you?*

# 7.

# The *Good News* Is *Bad News* To The Flesh *or* DEATH Always Precedes RESURRECTION

**Many rejoice at the thought of salvation**, as indeed they should. How wonderful it is that we can literally be transformed within by a supernatural act performed by a supernatural God!

Yet in our zeal to receive for ourselves and to proclaim to others the benefits and blessings that are in Jesus Christ, we can easily overlook the absolute *necessity* of accepting and stressing His demands. We must recognize not only His promises and blessings, but also His *conditions* for receiving them!

**Remember that it was the Lord Jesus Who said,**
"If any person wills to come after Me, let him deny himself — that is, disown himself, forget, lose sight of himself and his own interests, refuse and give up himself — and take up his cross daily, and follow Me." [Luke 9:23; Amplified Version]. Then again, "If anyone comes to Me and does not hate his [own] father and mother [that is, in the sense of indifference to or relative disregard for them in comparison with his attitude toward God] and likewise his wife and children and brothers and sisters, [yes] and even his own life also, he cannot be My disciple...so then, whoever of you does not forsake — renounce, surrender claim to, give up, say goodbye to — all that he has cannot be My disciple." [Luke 14:26, 33; Amplified].

The Apostle Paul, writing to Jesus' followers, said, "So

then, brethren, we are debtors, but not to the flesh — we are not obligated to our carnal nature — to live [a life ruled by the standards set up by the dictates] of the flesh. For if you live according to [the dictates of] the flesh you will surely die. But if through the power of the [Holy] Spirit you are habitually putting to death — making extinct, deadening — the [evil] deeds prompted by the body, you shall [really and genuinely] live forever." [Romans 8:13; Amplified].

From these and numerous other Scriptures we can see that God means business when it comes to His high and holy expectations of those that are His. Indeed, the *Good News* — the Gospel of Jesus Christ — with its proclamation and power to free people from their bondages of self-seeking and sin — is *bad news* to "the flesh," which is "our 'natural' reasoning and desires apart from a relationship with God."

God demands absolute consecration to His will and plans. The very essence of sin is the existence of another's will in opposition to God's, therefore God will not tolerate His creatures living independently of His will. He has this right, you know. Besides, God is so good and benevolent, His demanding our complete acceptance of His will is always for our best good.

**Still, some may object**

to this presentation of the Gospel, having not been taught these requirements. But that does not change the facts. It is truly sad and tragic that much that has been passed off as true Christianity is nothing more than a watered-down version at best of the genuine article, men interpreting to the liking of other men what they want or perceive the Gospel to be. Real, revealed Christianity [See Matthew 16:17] demands a turning away from *our* pursuits and interests to give ourselves fully to God for *His* pursuits and interests.

It is unacceptable to God for us to just add Him to the loves of our hearts. No! He demands that He be *the* love of our hearts.

As one familiar saying goes, "If He is not Lord of all, then He is not Lord at all!"

This is an indispensable part of the Gospel of Jesus Christ.

"For the grace of God that brings deliverance from sin and its curses has appeared to all men, teaching us to say 'No!' to all ungodliness and worldly passions, and to live self-controlled, upright and godly lives in this present age, while we wait for the blessed hope — the glorious appearing of our great God and Savior, Jesus Christ, Who gave Himself on our behalf that He might redeem us (that is, purchase our freedom) from all wickedness and purify for Himself a people that are His very own, eager to do what is good." [Titus 2:11-14; based on NIV].

Yes, even in view of God's goodness and thoughtfulness towards us in that He has so often lavished blessings upon us beyond our needs, His ultimate purpose for us is for His glory. As 1 Peter 2:9 says: "...you are a chosen people, a royal priesthood, a holy nation, a people belonging to God, that you may declare the praises of Him Who called you out of darkness into His wonderful light. [Based on NIV].

**And how will He fulfill His ultimate purpose, for His glory?**

By revealing Himself to, in, and through us.

God's promises to us were not designed to develop a selfish "gimme" consciousness of self-fulfillment and aggrandizement. Instead, His very great and precious promises to us have been given so that by them we might become sharers and partakers of the divine nature and escape the corruption that is in the world because of lust [2 Peter 1:3-4], which has self-fulfillment and selfishness at its core.

It is certain, God's call of life to us is also the death sentence of the fleshly nature with its selfish, self-glorifying demands upon ourselves and others. Only as we die to our own life can we be reborn to share in Jesus Christ's resurrection life!

The Good News *is* bad news to the flesh!

*Death always precedes resurrection...*

**I used to drive by what seemed to be a barren field.**

It looked tilled and furrowed, but totally desolate. One night while passing it, as usual it appeared to be barren and dead. However, the very next morning, as I went by I could see a blanket of new, green shoots all over it. The field that had appeared to be barren, dead, and desolate had in actuality been going through a preparation to burst forth with life! Beneath the surface, the miracle and wonder of life had taken root, grown, and was born, as it were, out of death. Though hidden from observation for awhile as it developed, the life within the soil could not be contained. The field, instead of being a tomb of barrenness and death, was actually a womb of fertility and life — resurrection life — so to speak.

The seeds that had been sown in the field had not been sown in vain. Although it seemed as though no seeds had even been planted, much less taken root, they had totally fulfilled their purpose by dying so that a new form and expression of life could come forth. As Jesus said, "...unless a kernel of wheat falls to the ground and dies, it remains only a single seed. But if it dies, it produces many seeds..." [John 12:24; NIV].

As with the field, so with those who are faithful unto death to the Lord. Though we may appear to be dead and barren, the Lord is doing a great, secret work within us that shall soon be manifested! Hallelujah!!

Furthermore, those who are "faithful unto death" (and this can mean more than just physical death) will be given the crown of life. [Revelation 2:10b]. Our obedient dying to self and all else that does not pertain to the kingdom of life and godliness will be the "soil" in which the resurrection life of the Son of God will be developed and seen.

So don't be discouraged:

*Death always precedes resurrection!*

# 8.

# Services, Rituals, And Plans

**Many so called "Christian" gatherings or "services"** are often declarations that we don't really believe in a God Who desires and is able to intervene in our affairs. Void of the reality of the Spirit of God in their lives, many have settled for and promoted rituals and a predictable, man-controlled, so called "order of worship."(???)

Are we threatened by the fact that God may have plans that differ from ours; a God who by His free, sovereign, non-chaotic yet unpredictable Spirit may take us to heights we've never known?

This, however, is the essence of Christianity — a Living God intervening with love, wisdom, and discipline into the intricacies of His creation. Therefore, we should look to Him, not man, when we gather with the saints, allowing Him to express Himself in and through us.

Otherwise, our profession will be empty — lacking reality.

**We claim to believe in God.**

Well, are the things of God more to us than mere fairy tales? Are they merely enjoyable, interesting, or entertaining to think about, but not to be taken seriously?

Do our lives and our gatherings bear the refreshing mark of spontaneity that comes as a result of anticipating what our Living Father might do next? Or are they marked with the stale, dead spirit of predictable, religious froth and foam — "dead" in its expression of truly spiritual life, and void of actual real life effectiveness?

Let's not forget that Satan is religious. How he loves pomp and circumstance, void of true, spiritual food!

But the Living God searches for hearts right before Him, regardless of a lack of religious structure. As a matter of fact, such hearts may even have only a very limited insight into spiritual matters. They may even be struggling fiercely in the grips of sin!...

**Remember what Jesus told the religious,** hypocritical, proud and self-sufficient Jewish chief priests and elders one day regarding themselves, prostitutes, and tax collectors [The tax collectors that Jesus referred to were Jewish agents of the oppressive Roman government who had the reputation of stealing from their fellow Jews by overtaxing them and pocketing the difference. They were hated by most of the other Jews.]: "...I tell you the truth, the tax collectors and the prostitutes are entering the Kingdom of God ahead of you. For John came to you to show you the way of righteousness, and you did not believe him, but the tax collectors and the prostitutes did." [Matthew 21:31b-32a; based on NIV].

You see, the Lord seeks hearts hungry for Truth, hungry for Him; hearts willing to admit their utter helplessness and brokenness apart from Him; hearts not trying to impress Him with theatrical displays of religious form. Such religious antics at best only symbolize the realities He desires, expects, and has enabled us to walk in.

**_Away_ with games! _Away_ with pretense!**

_Away_ with fleshly performances ladened with the expected formalities and demonstrations of the religious status quo!

Who are we trying to impress, anyway?

If the answer is one another (as it just might be), then we have our reward — we'll have none from Him. However, if it is true that in the depths of our beings we desire to follow Him, live in Him, and reveal Him to His creation, then let us settle it in our hearts once and for all, if possible, that we will not live according to men's expectations, but God's.

Now I'm not advocating being a "wild-hair," a radical, a

renegade or dissenter just for the thrill of controversy or strife. No, a thousand times no! Rather, I am encouraging us to simply put the Lord before our face — not the tenets and expectations of men.

Oftentimes in doing so, we will find ourselves pleasing others, while at other times at great odds with others, perhaps even our brothers and sisters in Christ. But neither really matters (though of course contention and differences cause sadness and grief), because we learn to look to Him for approval or disapproval — not others, not even ourselves. [1 Corinthians 4:3-4].

Whether people agree with us or not isn't the issue — pleasing *Him* is.

## Jesus Our Example:
## He was totally abandoned to God.

Like Jesus in response to His mother and brothers calling Him from outside [Mark 3:31-35], or in His response to an urgent message regarding Lazarus being sick [John 11:6], or with His seeming lack of concern, being fast asleep during a tremendous storm at sea [Mark 4:37-38], our lives, if we truly live unto God alone, will take on an apparent indifference or "holy apathy," so to speak, of which we need not be apologetic or afraid.

For if we truly believe in the God of our Lord Jesus Christ as a living, approachable Person that our Lord revealed, instead of a figment of a religious imagination, we can rest in the confidence that even His sometimes puzzling and seemingly cold or indifferent ways of leading are laced in His wisdom and love. Think about that awhile...

## Imagine how very simple our lives can be if we will live to only please God!

Then we will no longer fret over the fickleness of changing human emotions and viewpoints. On the contrary, we will then be always living in the constant knowledge that God is with us, watching us, and leading us, and it is to Him ultimately that we must give an account.

We must only keep our hearts tender towards all others,

not allowing this insight to be perverted into an occasion to sin by developing a cocky, mean, unteachable attitude. If God can rebuke a prophet through a jackass (remember Balaam and his donkey? [Numbers 22:28-30]), He certainly can speak to us through whomever or whatever He chooses! So we must stay open to God and draw Him forth from those we can, always remembering that *He* is our pursuit and path.

Let's be done with *our* services, rituals, and plans. Instead, let us lay hold of the Lord, determining to do only what He says to do, living by "every word that comes forth from the mouth of God." [Deuteronomy 8:3; Matthew 4:4]. Then and only then will we experience the fullness of the manifestation of His presence in our midst and see the body of Christ come to complete maturity.

*Not our way, but God's Way, moment to moment.*

### Revelation — Not Interpretation

(a song)

Chorus:
*The Lord has not called us to interpretation,*
*but called us to a higher realm of revelation!*

*Man's wisdom does not impress the Lord.*
*To Him our thoughts are futile and foolish.*
*So why do we think we'll make Him smile*
*by our programs and rituals and plans?*

*Oh, we better listen to the Holy Ghost —*
*His ways are so much higher,*
*and be done with our man-made walk*
*that's destined for the fire.*

*For God has called us to Himself*
*where we cease from our own labors*
*and walk in His thoughts and His life and His love,*

*and stop thinkin' we can do Him favors.*

*Oh, the Lord wants us to come to know Him*
*very intimately,*
*but He'll not move like I know He would*
*while we're doin' our own thing —*
*claimin' that it's His —*
*doin' our own thing.*

Chorus:
*The Lord has not called us to interpretation,*
*but called us to a higher realm of revelation!*

# 9.

# Testimony

**After hearing about Jesus Christ** and His ever present love, I came to a time in my life when I personally confronted Him. He required me to look to Him as my only hope and source of salvation from the wrath and judgments of God. He made it clear that apart from Him, I did not have the desire nor the ability to pursue God or to secure salvation.

I saw that I deserved God's wrath and punishment for rebellion against Him. But Jesus had taken my place, becoming my substitute. Therefore, I was to cast myself totally upon His mercy, accepting what He had already accomplished on my behalf through His victorious death and resurrection.

However, I did not come to the realization of these facts with ease, but rather with great pain, for first I became totally convinced of my desperate situation: I justly deserved God's judgment of damnation and wrath.

## I knew the "Word of God," but not the God of the Word.

Oh, I was full of much head knowledge about the Lord. I could quote much Scripture by memory. There were many who said that I had blessed them with my ministry before all this took place. Nevertheless, God showed me what was probably only a glimpse of the condition of my heart and how really empty I was of Him, though I was so full of other things.

This was when I first began to realize that someone could be full of knowledge of "the Word of God" without knowing the God of the Word.

My intense torments continued and increased in their vehemence, and this terror was unrelenting for about six months. There was trauma by day and nightmares by night.

One thing that was dealt a mighty blow in me was doubt as to God's existence. I had but a taste of what it will be like for many as they stand in dread and terror before the Holy, Living God on the awesome Day of Judgment [Revelation 21:11-15], yet I saw clearly that there would definitely be no atheists!

**I probably would be unable to fully convey the trauma and absolute terror that engulfed me**

as I realized I was helpless in myself to escape what I knew was the just condemnation of God. It was as though I had stood before the throne of God and had been justly condemned to Hell forever. I literally wept and wailed and gnashed my teeth, and often screamed out to God, begging Him to have mercy on my soul.

Sometimes, I even banged my head against the floor or wall in total hopelessness, despair, and torment. Paul wrote in Romans 7:18 that he knew that nothing good dwelled in his flesh. The loathsomeness of my heart and state of being became so real to me that I believe I could have written that verse with just as much conviction as Paul.

All my knowledge, pat answers, and neat little clichés were shown to be futile when not energized by the Spirit of God, as I began to see that I was undeserving of God's mercy and help, but oh!, so very helpless and needy.

**I sincerely and intensely searched**

for help and consolation from other people, but to no avail. As a matter of fact, many times when others would try to help me, it seemed as though they were skimming a rock on the surface of the ocean, and I was sitting on the ocean floor — far from being affected by them.

All doubt as to the reality of Jesus' own claims to be the source of life, deliverance, and transformation for me and all of humanity disappeared completely as I became fully aware that He alone was sufficient and able to deliver me from my plight.

So began an earnest and intense seeking after Him, crying out to Him for mercy. I came to the place where I felt convinced that there was no hope, and oh!, how awful that feeling is! Nevertheless, I continued crying out to God because I knew that there was no higher appeal to whom I could beg and plead for mercy.

### And then, one morning

I awoke from sleep and immediately became aware that something was drastically different. It was as though a great weight and burden had been lifted off of me. At the same time, I recognized that it was the work of the Lord Jesus.

He had set me free!!

It was truly a sovereign work of God, for no man could ever even touch the pain or turmoil that I had lived through those several months. The Lord Jesus, with the same power with which He rose from the grave, set my life free — dramatically yet tenderly — from its constant torments.

### Jesus is Lord!

And now my own experience attests to this fact: Jesus is, as He said, the Only Way and the Lord Supreme. The way for us to live a full, worthwhile, and victorious life is for Him to live His life in and through us. He sends His Spirit to dwell within us when we turn from our selfish, ego-worshipping lifestyles and turn to Him, acknowledging Him as our only Hope and Lord. He desires for us to long for, ask for, and receive a constant filling and flow of His Holy Spirit.

The Lord Jesus is truly Head over all things. He stands forever as the source and dispenser of life as it was intended to be experienced. Ruling supremely over creation, He is able and willing to give anyone a new identity — yes, a new existence. And (glorious thought!) as we choose to

live our life within the longing to know Him better, looking
to Him as our life, a miracle of transformation takes place.
We find ourselves being changed from within to become
just like Him.

## What a metamorphosis!

From being one manifesting and leading to death, we
now can – in a continuously greater way — reveal in our
person His very life and character.

Then, as this transformation becomes mature, just as
He said, "If you've seen Me, you've seen the Father," each
of us will be able to boldly yet humbly say, "If you've seen
me, you've seen the Son!"

## Testimony (a song)

*I heard about His eyes so clear*
*and full of undying love so dear.*
*Then I heard His voice calling oh so sweet,*
*"Come, lost one, come unto Me."*

*You know it wasn't long ago that I discovered I was lost.*
*And no man could help or pay the cost*
*to set me free from misery*
*except Jesus, Who paid the price for you and me.*

*So I cried to Him, "Come and save me, dear Lord.*
*I'm helpless, I see. Lord, it's only You that I need."*
*Then He stretched forth His hands — strong,*
*and so very able to save —*
*and He redeemed my life, so that now I say,*

*"Jesus is the Way, the Only Way, and He is Lord.*
*If it's peace that you need, friend,*
*He's what you've been looking for.*
*He's the Lord of life and evermore shall be...*
*King of kings, Lord of lords;*
*He'll give you a new life and what's more:*

*As you look into His face, you'll become like Him,*
*just like Him, changed from within,*
*to become...*
*just like Him."*

# 10.

# The Quest

**As I think back on days gone by,** I recall many times when I frantically tried to get more out of life. I tried all sorts of different things and experiences, but they left me feeling empty and defeated, and did not bring rest to my troubled heart and mind.

In more sublime, contemplative, serious moods, I would even try to find a meaning for my life; a reason or purpose for my existence. But again, my search, though often more refined and even "religious," did not satisfy my needs, nor did it quench my inward hunger and thirst.

**Even after becoming one of God's children,**
His incomprehensible peace, the power and real experience of His life, and "the rest" to which He has called His people [Hebrews 3:13-4:11] were missing from my experience to a great extent. Too often I was not victorious over the pressures and realities of this present life. Also, God's promise of a life of continuous victory, clear understanding and insight, and supernatural peace of mind and heart seemed to evade me.

About this time I was becoming acutely aware that the "something more" I needed and longed for would never be found in the confines of religious forms and rituals. So my heart began to cry out for reality and substance; not just the empty shell of pretentious, religious show, "put-on," and practices. I began to see that God has always been working towards the furtherance of a unified, eternal kingdom with His Son Jesus as its *only* Head.

Over the centuries, however, a many-headed monster has been developed. It is man-made, man-governed, and destined for destruction.

**The body of Christ does not consist of a Baptist arm, a Lutheran leg, a Catholic foot and so forth.**

The Lord never intended these and other kinds of carnal divisions that we see in the Church. No, each of us who truly belong to Jesus "...are all parts of one body and members one of another" [Ephesians 4:25b; Amplified], in need of each and every other person who belongs to the Lord. There is not to be any party, sectarian spirit that separates us from one another. The Spirit of God said through Paul the apostle in 1 Corinthians 1:10: "...I urge and entreat you, brethren, by the name of our Lord Jesus Christ, that all of you be in perfect harmony, and full agreement in what you say, and that there be no dissensions or factions or divisions among you; but that you be perfectly united in your common understanding and in your opinions and judgments." [Amplified Version].

Separatist attitudes such as: "I belong to Cephas;" "I belong to Paul;" "I belong to *this* group, and you belong to *that* group," are not to be tolerated at all. [1 Corinthians 1:12-13]. Galatians 5:19-20 reveal that such actions are born of the flesh, and not of the Holy Spirit: "Now the doings of the flesh are obvious: ...enmity, strife, jealousy, anger (ill temper), selfishness, divisions (dissensions), party spirit (factions, sects with peculiar opinions, heresies...." [Based on Amplified Version]. And the somber warning of verse 21 shows how displeasing to the Lord such activities are: "...I warn you beforehand, just as I did previously, that those who do such things shall not inherit the Kingdom of God." [Based on Amplified].

The divisions we see testify to the fact that we have clung more to the ways and the thinking of men than we have to the Lord, because these divisions are most definitely not His will and they grieve His Spirit deeply.

While I realized that many precious people were dedicated to man-made and man-led organizations, and often with pure motives though clouded vision, I nonetheless also saw that

**"he that remains on a sinking ship will with that
ship sink."**

Regardless of how pretty or crowded a "ship" is, if it's
going down, we're going down too if we don't flee it — the
sooner the better!

Now some may argue that the Lord has them involved
in this system of man to reach others in it. They might
also say that it is perhaps for only a "season," and I'm not
writing this for vain controversy, but I can certainly say by
the Word of the Lord that all our hearts must be set
completely on the establishing of the Kingdom of God —
promoting God's plans, not man's.

To further illustrate, consider this true story. We'll call
it :

**"The Doomed Dynasty":**

Many years ago, an heir of a powerful king became the
very best of friends with someone who was both a servant
in the king's court and a mighty warrior. It seemed as
though their destinies were fixed, with the heir becoming
king and his friend remaining a loyal subject. However,
such was not the case. Instead, the Lord God had chosen
the servant warrior to become king, because he had proven
himself faithful to the Lord while the king had stubbornly
rebelled against the Lord.

The heir of the disobedient king accepted the Lord's
decree wholeheartedly because he loved the Lord and he
loved his friend. He even discussed with his servant friend
how he would reign next to him when the Lord had placed
his friend on the throne.

But even though the heir knew that his father's dynasty
was under God's judgment; even though he knew that his
friend was the Lord's choice as the next monarch of the
kingdom, he nonetheless chose to remain with his father
and within the structure of the doomed dynasty.

**Sadly, one fateful day,**

the king and his son were killed in battle. Had the heir, Jonathan, left his father's cursed court and joined forces with David, the Lord's chosen, he probably would have seen the fulfillment of his dream of sitting next to his dear friend in the newly established kingdom. [See 1 Samuel 18:1-4; 23:15-18; 31:1-6].

He that has ears to hear, let him hear!

## Bless the Living God!

He's begun a work of opening the eyes of my heart to see the reality of His eternal, unseen as yet kingdom. How wonderful is the truth that the Almighty Son of the Living God has joined Himself to me in a marriage of our Spirits that enables Him to express His eternal, resurrection power in and through my being!

Now I've begun to see that truly He has become my ability to endure all of life's tests. He has become the source and spring of my life itself, and as I rely on and obey Him, I experience freedom from all sin. He gives not only commands, but also the power to obey them.

## My active willingness coupled with God's power enables me to do all His will.

My life has become both simplified and enlarged. It has been simplified by ridding my mind of all the clutter of religious formulas, which are man-made substitutes for the leading and power of the Holy Spirit. It has been enlarged by the recognition of my need for His precious Presence to be united with me, fill me, and flow through me.

As I cease from leaning to my own understanding, and focus on Him and my relationship to Him, I am led more into His rest. This produces a childlike peace, and He is free to be God in and through me.

## This is the only way to walk in His best.

I thank God for showing me that His dealings with me are to one end: that I would seek and come to know Jesus Christ in an ever deepening and more insightful way.

I'm not called to preach a pet dogma, doctrine or creed,

but Jesus Christ Himself — eternal, incarnate, crucified, risen, reigning, and returning!

He is the Beginning and the End — the A and the Z. He is the Life. He is the Destiny...

*HE is the Quest!*

## The Quest (a song)

*In all my frantic wanderings*
*I never found within*
*the peace of God, His life or rest,*
*and freedom from all sin.*

*Throughout my quest for fullness*
*I could never seem to find*
*the life that He had promised —*
*full of light and peace of mind.*

*But now (and by His grace, I know),*
*I'm starting to behold*
*the way of peace and sweet release*
*and freedom for the soul.*

*For now, though dimly viewed at times,*
*by His grace I can see,*
*the Christ of God, victorious, by His Spirit, lives in me.*
*For by His Spirit's wooing me from folly unto Him,*
*I gave myself unto Him, and He came to dwell within.*

*But with that the story's not complete,*
*and I cannot end it there.*
*For although being His,*
*I was distraught by life's affairs.*
*And so, though He had pardoned me,*
*I yet still longed for more;*
*and sought Him for reality — not ritualistic forms.*

*So now, bless God, He's started*
*to illumine my heart's eyes*
*and remove their scales, and part the veil*
*wherein His glory lies.*
*I've begun to see "Immanuel" — "God with us" —*
*now lives within; and He's my stay, **He** is my life,*
*my freedom from all sin.*

*So now I choose to enter and abide within His rest*
*and cease from self-willed wanderings.*
*His best is in His rest,*
*and **He** is all the Quest.*

# Our Relationship With God Deepens

*"The person who has My commands and keeps them*
*is the one who [really] loves Me,*
*and whoever really loves Me*
*will be loved by My Father.*
*And I [too] will love him*
*and will show (reveal, manifest) Myself to him —*
*I will let Myself be clearly seen by him*
*and make Myself real to him."*
***Jesus***
***[John 14:21; Amplified]***

*"Those whom I love*
*I rebuke and discipline..."*
***Jesus***
***[Revelation 3:19a; NIV]***

*"...If a person [really] loves Me,*
*he will keep My word — obey My teaching;*
*and My Father will love him,*
*and We will come to him and make Our home*
*(abode, special dwelling place) with him."*
***Jesus***
***[John 14:23; Amplified]***

# 11.

# Israel Fought — God Wrought

**The sun broke the darkness** with the first rays of dawn. As it gained in its splendor, one could see the expanse of opposing armies spreading across the land, ready and eager for battle.

Finally, the face off was over, and with trumpet blasts and an earthshaking roar the two armies raced towards each other, eager for the conflict and the thrill of victory.

One army was from one of the nations of the land of Canaan, the other was the Israeli army under the command of Joshua. Amidst clouds of dust, the searing heat of the sun, and the cries and shouts of men, the two armies fought with deadly fury and intent.

**On and on they fought,**

hour after hour, even till the sun began waning in its strength and the first indications of dusk came. More than once during the day the Jewish warriors had sensed a resurgence and renewal of strength when it seemed they would grow weary. Their opposers' strength, however, ebbed away.

At long last, the fierce battle was over, and the amazing outcome was evident: The destruction and carnage of the Canaanite army was complete — not a man was left alive, while in the Jewish ranks, not a man was missing!

Back in their camp, reunited with their families and loved ones, the Jewish nation lifted their hands and voices in praise to God as they fell on their faces before Him in adoration, worship, and thankfulness. "O Lord God, You did it! You wrought this great victory today by the hand of Your servants! You won the victory! You deserve all the praise!"

[Now although this specific story is fictional, the events and attitudes revealed in it are based on historical fact. See Joshua 6:16; 8:1-2; 10:7-10, 25, 32, 42; 11:1-9; 23:8-10. Also see Numbers 31:49.].

Isn't it something in this example, that though the Israeli army fought so hard and furiously, they gave all the glory to God, declaring Him the victor? Most analysts would have said the Jewish army had won the victory. After all, they were out in the scorching sun all day engaging in the weariness of fierce combat. And surely couldn't some of the credit for their victories be ascribed to Joshua's military genius in directing brilliant tactical maneuvers, or because of military superiority?

No, the Israelites knew better! They were aware that their great military conquests were not due to any human intelligence, power, or prowess. On the contrary, they were probably very conscious of the fact that the nations they defeated were actually greater in numbers and might than they were. [Deuteronomy 7:7-8; 11:22-25].

The Jews walked triumphant and undefeated as they moved in a principle of the Kingdom of God that is just as applicable for God's people today as it was for them those many centuries ago:

**Apart from Him, God's people are helpless against their enemies. However,**

as they walk in dependent obedience to Him, acknowledging their need of Him and His ability and willingness to meet their needs, something wonderful happens. They exchange their inabilities for His abilities, and their weaknesses for His strengths! This is how they walk in the victory of the Lord that He works within and that they must then "work out."

Let's take a closer look at this: The people of God choose and determinedly set forth to do His will, looking steadfastly and expectantly to Him, knowing that only by His help can they ever experience victory. Responding to their faith in Him, He then enables His people to fully accomplish His intents.

## Beautiful, isn't it?

God supplies energy, wisdom, yes, the complete ability to fulfill any task that He requires His people to do. Unfortunately, oftentimes many of His people fall into one of two traps...

On the one hand, many try to accomplish what they think is the will of God, without nurturing and maintaining an ongoing intimacy with and dependency on Him, and thus they fail miserably. They even *start* from a point of failure: You cannot please God (no matter how outwardly successful your deeds may seem) without a complete reliance on Him, allowing Him to inspire and enable, and thus receive the glory.

On the other hand, some get a revelation of God's power and glory, then acquiesce and don't fight in the face of challenges, thinking that since the Lord is the Almighty God, He will bring victory in and through their lives if He wishes. Believe me, He does! But, as we've mentioned, the Lord has chosen to bring about His victory through us with our cooperation. You see, we are called to be co-laborers — fellow workers — with God. [1 Corinthians 3:9].

## It is not all us, and it is not all God!

It is us doing our part, and God doing His part.

He has chosen us as major components in the accomplishing of His will, but we are not called to do so without Him. Indeed we cannot. Recall Jesus' words, "...apart from Me you can do nothing." [John 15:5b; NAS].

*Our choice coupled with God's power enables us to fully accomplish God's will.* The two go perfectly hand in hand.

We should learn from the Israelites of old, drawing from their experiences. They, like us, had a specific mission from God. They accomplished His will the same way we must — by firmly relying on the Lord as they eagerly pursued His will. Such faith is always met with the sufficiency of God.

Let us never forget:

*Israel fought — God wrought!*

# 12.

# Come Forth, You Joshuas!

**Moses and his young assistant** and protégé, Joshua, entered, as they frequently did, into the designated "tent of meeting." Here the most awesome and incredible meetings occurred, for here the mortal confronted the immortal, the limited encountered the limitless: Man met face to face with God his Creator. Moses conversed with God as one would communicate with a friend — intimately, candidly, and with mutual love and respect.

After Moses completed his dialogue with the Most High, he left the "tent of meeting" in his usual manner — alone. For although Joshua would accompany Moses into this special tent, he would not leave with him. The Scripture tells us that Moses would return to the camp, but the young man Joshua would remain. [Exodus 33:11].

Ah, can you imagine what went on within Joshua? Can you sense the longing he must have had in his heart for the intimate acquaintance with the Living God? What a wonder it must have been for him to just sit there, perhaps, or lay stretched out on his face, basking in the immediate and manifest presence of God. At such times he probably contemplated on the goodness, greatness, and mystique of this invisible God Who found delight in conversing and having fellowship with His creature, man.

## Notice the focus of Joshua and Jesus:

Joshua was Moses' successor in the leadership of the Israelites, and his hunger for and fascination with God Himself was the secret of his extraordinary leadership capacities.

He was not just a man groomed after Moses' stead, a

warrior trained in the weapons of war, whose arms were strong because of training. Beyond that he was a man who loved his God and who longed to be in God's presence. Therein was the Lord pleased, and therein was Joshua used to do exploits.

Remember, also, when Jesus was baptized at the Jordan River. The heavens were opened and John the Baptist saw the Holy Spirit descend from Heaven in bodily form like a dove to rest upon Jesus. God the Father then spoke from Heaven, saying, "This is My beloved Son, in Whom I am well-pleased." [Matthew 3:17b; NAS].

### And with what was He pleased?

It wasn't with any great, miraculous work, for Jesus had not yet performed one miracle. It wasn't with some lofty sermon or teaching, for Jesus had not begun His public proclaiming of the Kingdom. It wasn't with any of the things that many of us followers of Jesus Christ have often got caught up in seeking, thinking that if we were involved in some "great" (by our definition) or so called "spiritual" work we would then be really pleasing to our God.

No, Jesus was pleasing to His Father simply because He put His Father first in everything. He was consumed with love for God Himself!

Therefore, He was consumed with a determination to obey and please His Father in every circumstance. He walked habitually, constantly, in union and communion with God, and had but one pursuit — His Father's will. [John 6:38; also John 5:19, 30].

Furthermore, this passionate devotion not only made Jesus pleasing to Father, it also procured the miracles and ministry that followed.

### First Relationship — *Then* Ministry:

*It wasn't ministry that produced relationship — it was relationship that produced ministry!*

This is the real heartcry of the Father. This has always been the way of the Kingdom of God. God, through relationship with His people, intimate and ongoing, establishes them as His true ministers and as "living letters" [2 Corinthians 3:2] read by all men.

### Relationship — Not Religion:

Religion, in its vain attempt to produce sonship, has created a bastard product by merely teaching concepts and interpretations. In effect, religion says, "Here are the shoes of a true minister of the New Covenant. This is the way you are supposed to be; this is what you are supposed to do if you are a prophet, a pastor, or what have you."

But the Kingdom of God is not so...

God so works in a person's being whom He has apprehended that the *person* defines what the call is, not the other way around!

For example, one truly called by God to be an apostle will define true apostleship by everything that they are and do. It is true that as they walk in union with God they will be developed in their maturity and calling, and God will utilize other servants of His in their life. However, in them is the Scripture fulfilled that says, "...the anointing you received from Him remains in you, and you do not need anyone to teach you." [1 John 2:27a; based on NIV].

Others may share wonderful truths with them, and may even impart spiritual gifts to them. [Romans 1:11]. Nevertheless, in the truest sense of the word, "apostleship," or any other calling from God, for that matter, will not be "learned" from others. Our calling is like being a male or female: It's something that one *is* — not something that one *learns,* per se.

It is just as plausible to think that if a female were taught how to be a male, that would make her one, as it is to believe that to attempt to teach someone "how to" fulfill a certain calling in God would mean that they truly had the calling and the enablement to fulfill it. If it was not "in them," "what they were," it would be, at best, a tragic act.

### In the Kingdom, what a person *is* is what counts, not just what they know.

A doctor may "practice" medicine, a lawyer may

"practice" law, but a servant of God does not merely "practice" his or her calling. Though "by reason of use" of their senses (Hebrews 5:14) and a disciplined commitment of obedience to God they help to make their "calling and election sure" (2 Peter 1:3-11), someone's calling is something they are within — it is their "essence" — and not merely a discipline that they develop.

In short: In the Kingdom, what a person is by nature, not merely what they learn through memorization or rote, is what counts.

**If we have ears to hear, then we need to listen, comprehend and do — by *being!***

True sonship belongs to those who are led by the Spirit of God. [Romans 8:14]. This is speaking of intimate and ongoing relationship. Come forth, therefore, you Joshuas, and lay hold of your God! Come forth, you who would walk the way of the Son in obedience to His God and our God, His Father and our Father!

For this is an hour of action and mobilization...

The Lord shall establish His covenant in the earth, and men will see and witness the testimony of the Most High. For the Spirit of prophecy shall sweep God's people. The testimony shall come forth of Jesus Christ. For such is the Spirit of prophecy — the testimony, the declaring forth, glorification, and revealing of Jesus Christ.

**We are to be active participants.**

We have a part and a role. We have a choice — and are not automatons. As we choose to lay hold of and know the Lord, therein shall we do exploits and take the land, just as Joshua did because of his choice to remain in the "tent of meeting" that he might draw closer to the One Who had called and loved him.

Yes, they that know their God in this hour shall do exploits! For the Lord has declared that this is the hour of demonstration, not that flesh should be exalted, but that flesh might be abased and God alone be glorified.

Let us be encouraged, therefore, in this hour, to stir up

that which the Lord our God has deposited within us. For if we are one of His, the Lord has chosen to use us, but He looks for a reciprocal response:

**Do we *choose* to be used?**

It is our CHOICE coupled with God's POWER that enables us to accomplish God's WILL.

So do we choose to be a part of this marvelous flow, this rising tide of the Spirit? We cannot contain it, but we can get in over our heads and go with it! [See Ezekiel 47:2-5].

For God has called us to something bigger than ourselves. He has called us to something bigger than the local assembly, yes, bigger than just what we might perceive on a world-wide basis.

The Lord would have us know and be participants in the eternal purposes of God. The reason for this is so that when this thing is wrapped up, and the heavens are laid aside as a garment, and the Lord God creates new heavens and a new earth, we will have had an active role and still be with Him, participating in seeing the increase of the Son's government having no end.

Therefore, let it be settled in our hearts that we will not be people of mere repetition and rote, but be people in love with our God! For the Lord will take us down paths that are well known, and then suddenly He'll take us down ones we've not yet experienced.

**But this is reserved for those**

who listen, and long, and love:

For those who listen for His voice...

who long for His fellowship...

and who love Him with *all* of their being.

# 13.

# The Chair

**Years ago I walked into a huge tent** full of many chairs. As I looked around, the Spirit of God flashed this into my mind:

Imagine a very large tent or hall with hundreds, maybe even thousands of chairs. Let's say that each chair represented a bit of understanding of the things that pertain to the Kingdom of God: this chair being a certain gift of the Spirit, this chair representing wisdom, etc.

Now imagine how painstaking and ultimately frustrating it would be if we were called to study each chair in detail, to the finest degree, even using a microscope. Such a task would be extremely wearisome and disturbing. Not only would the study be grueling, but even deciding which chair to study next would weigh heavily upon a sensitive, seeking soul. "Am I studying the right 'chair' (that is, 'the right doctrine or emphasis') at the present time?"

**A frustrating scenario indeed.**

But let's suppose that someone stops us and leads us to one certain, spectacular chair, encouraging us to study it and it alone. Suddenly our task would seem incredibly less wearisome, wouldn't you say?

Now suppose that we study this chair ever so diligently and carefully, and, looking up, to our astonishment we find that we intuitively know all there is to know about a whole section of chairs that seemed impossible to fully know! Then, as we continue to study this one particular chair, we come to see that we know all there is to know about another group of chairs!

### What am I saying?

Simply this:

That one, extraordinary chair represents Jesus Christ.

As we pour our lives into the pursuit of the intimate, personal knowledge of *Him,* and not just His ways and things *about* Him, we will find ourselves rewarded by His Spirit with insight and understanding of all we need to know. For in Jesus all the treasures of divine wisdom and knowledge lie "hidden" [Proverbs 2:7] — unseen and unknown to the casual passerby, but revealed by God's Spirit to those who hunger and thirst for righteousness. [Colossians 2:3].

### And how does He reveal these treasures to us?

By revealing Jesus the Christ.

Our hunger and thirst for righteousness will only be satisfied by knowing Him. As a matter of fact, *all* sincere and persistent quests for Truth will find their fulfillment in Him...

*Everything* we need to know is in the Lord Jesus!

Therefore, let's be caught up and in love with Him, with our hearts set and fixed on knowing Him.

# 14.

# Our Love And Pursuit — Is It For The Covenant Of The Lord Or The Lord Of The Covenant? *or* The Greater Includes The Lesser

**We can know the things of God and yet not know God.** However, it is true that the greater includes the lesser, and if we come to know God, we will understand the things of God.

Again, we definitely need to study the Scriptures, looking to the Lord to speak to us through them. [2 Timothy 2:15; 3:16-17]. However, we also need to always be aware to not settle for just an academic knowledge of the Scriptures without maintaining open hearts before the Lord. As a matter of fact, we can know many Scriptures and have concepts about applying them without knowing God, but if we know Him, we will automatically, by His nature within us, be led into a hunger for and correct knowledge of Scripture, as well as a proper outworking of it's principles.

The greater includes the lesser.

Similarly, many speak of "covenant" promises and relationship. They talk of God desiring that we lay hold of His covenant that we might secure all that He has promised us in it. But here again:

The greater includes the lesser...

## There is something higher than covenant:

It is relationship.

Now some may argue that this is a mute point, since the covenant is but the outworking and defining of the terms and blessings of relationship between God and His people. It is true that the covenants that God has made with His people throughout history have been linked to His love for them and a longing for relationship with them, but here is where I want us to again see that the greater includes the lesser...

## How saddened any husband would be if his beloved,

his bride, demanded and laid claim to promised provisions from him based on their marriage contract or "covenant." She may surely be entitled to these things in view of their relationship, and he may have promised her many things, but how disheartening and ultimately unfulfilling it would be if any part of their relationship was based on such an approach! How much more fulfilled, and yes, even more willing to give, a loving husband would be if his wife simply loved him for himself; not his provisions! He would delight in pouring his treasures and love upon such a woman who was deeply in love and devoted to him, and not his riches.

## Do you see the point?

The Living God loves His people deeply and tenderly. He doesn't mind blessing us with things, but far more His desire is to bless us with the knowledge of Himself that comes from intimacy with Him.

If we would but come to Him and love Him for Who He is, instead of at best having a mixed, polluted love that yearns for His blessings as much as it yearns for Him, we would find ourselves overtaken and ladened with His goodness and blessings. And, whether we had plenty of temporal blessings or few, we would be totally fulfilled and full of joy to know that we were in love with Him, and He with us.

Even so, God could entrust more temporal blessings and "things" to us if He knew that they would not become the objects of the pursuit of our hearts. He demands that He alone be the darling and consuming passion and pursuit of our hearts.

Let us not, therefore, settle for the covenant of the Lord, but let us settle only for the Lord of the covenant, for the greater includes the lesser!

Also, even our calling from God regarding ministry to others is to be an outgrowth of relationship with Him...

Consider our Lord Jesus. While truly loving people, He was not motivated to minister to others primarily out of love for them, but out of love for God His Father:

He only did what He saw the Father do.

He only said what He heard the Father say.

### He always did what pleased His Father.

His meat, His food, His sustenance was to do the will of His Father and complete the work that His Father had given Him to do. [See John 4:32; 5:19, 30; 7:28; 8:28-29; 12:49; Psalm 40:7-8; Hebrews 10:7].

Also, even our Lord's sacrificial death for His fallen creation was based on His love and commitment to God; not to His creation. [Luke 22:42].

As we consider these things, keep in mind that rather than weakening our love for our fellow man and duty before God, such a burning pursuit and commitment to God will only enhance and perfect all else. If we are truly committed to God, we will fulfill the wonderful, loving will of our Father far better than we ever could if our eyes and heart were set upon simply doing good things.

Also, our submission to one another will be pure and unfettered with the weights of human effort and enforcement if we will submit completely to the Lord. Then He will see to it that we are in right order and relationship with one another.

For it matters not what positions men hold [Galatians 2:6]. Rather, what matters is the position *He* holds within our beings.

## We must keep first things first!

All other things will fall into place if we love the Lord fully, singularly, and purely.

## Moses saw God's *ways* — not just His *acts.*

May our experience be as that of Moses instead of the other children of Israel. For it is written concerning the Lord, "He made known His *ways* to Moses, His *acts* to the children of Israel." [Psalm 103:7; NKJV]. "The Lord would speak to Moses face to face, as a man speaks with his friend." [Exodus 33:11a; NIV]. Moses witnessed the acts of the Lord, just as the rest of the children of Israel, but because of his intimacy with the Lord, Moses also was shown the Lord's ways, while the rest of God's people were not shown them.

This precious fellowship with the Living God that Moses enjoyed was not due just because of God's sovereign election. No, in Numbers 12:7, the Lord reveals that Moses was "...faithful in all My house." And because of that faithfulness, the Lord said in verse 8 regarding Moses, "With him I speak face to face, clearly and not in riddles; he sees the form of the Lord."

Moses maintained an intimacy with the Lord due to His faithful obedience, and because of that, he was privileged to have the Lord's ways revealed to him, and not just the Lord's acts!

## As with Moses, so it can be with us.

The Living God does desire that we see and participate in the demonstration of the Holy Spirit and of power. [1 Corinthians 2:4]. However, He is far more interested in having us develop and maintain intimate fellowship with Him and walk in "the secret of the Lord." [Psalm 25:14].

Furthermore, the Lord wants us to get our eyes off of His manifested power and "demonstration." His ideal is for His mighty acts to occur as a result or "offshoot" of our perception and pursuit of the higher goal — God Himself!

We are to pursue Him and enhance our perception of Him by seeking His face, refusing to do evil, and walking in obedience to Him. [See Psalm 91; Proverbs 8:13; and John 14:21, 23].

## Our First Priority:

The Lord Jesus said in Matthew 6:33, "...seek first the Kingdom of God and His righteousness, and all these things shall be added to you" [NKJV]. As we keep focused on Jesus, "the author and finisher of our faith" [Hebrews 12:2; NKJV], and the One in Whom is the Kingdom of God [Revelation 1:9; AMP, NAS, NIV], and the One Who also is "Our Righteousness" [Jeremiah 23:5-6; 33:16; 1 Corinthians 1:30], all that we could ever need will be ours. Plus, we will then also rest and rejoice in the most wonderful benefit of all: an intimate friendship, courtship, and union with God!

Yes, if we truly set our hearts on *Him,* and not just things *about* Him, all other things that we need will be ours...

*Truly, the Greater includes the lesser!*

[Also see Chapter 22: "Ready In Season And Out Of Season" for another example of the greater including the lesser — purity and prayer].

# 15.

# What Is Our Reason For Loving God?

**Are we committed to the Lord** and do we follow Him because we purely and simply love Him? Do we turn away from sin because of our love for God and His righteousness? Or do we do so merely because we fear God's painful judgments against sin and the torments of Hell?

If we could commit a pleasurable sin (one which our flesh would *love* to indulge in) and yet get away with it, with no repercussions or having to reap what we have sown, would we commit the sin? Or would we turn from it because we sincerely love righteousness?

Are we committed to the Lord Himself, or are we committed only to the position He maintains as God and Head over His creation? For instance, do we follow God because we love Him, or because between Him and Satan, God is the strongest of the two and the One Who shall always prevail?

**If it were possible**

that the Lord God could be defeated by Satan (a definite impossibility!), so that God was cast off of His throne and Satan ruled the universe, would we still follow, obey, and love the Lord, or would we follow and be devoted to Satan?

These are heavy, thought provoking and heart searching questions for many of us, but they are questions which can be used by the Spirit of God to expose the true condition of our hearts...

"O God, help us, enable us to love You purely, singularly, with all of our beings, unselfishly, for Your glory, regardless of circumstances!! In Jesus' name we pray to You, Father. Amen; may it be so."

Nothing short of an absolutely pure and simple devotion to God's Person will satisfy the type of intimacy and relationship He longs to have with us.

Let us pursue Him with a yearning to have Him do such a work within us that our love becomes and always stays pure, untainted, and holy. May we love righteousness and hate sin, not merely fear its consequences!

### What *is* our reason for loving God?

Do we really love Him, with absolute devotion, purity, and unselfishness? If not, we can do so, but only through the power of the life of the Son of God Himself.

He with us, in us, and through us can love this way. United with Him we can love as He loves!

Let us seek His face for this devotion of pure love.

# 16.

# Are We Meeting God, Or Are We Just Meeting?

**Upward the lone traveler climbed,** making an arduous journey up the mountain to its summit. The man, Moses, was about to have one of the most remarkable experiences any man has ever known. He was about to spend 40 days and nights, without food or water, in the immediate presence of the One Who created the worlds and Who now demanded an audience with him at the top of Mount Sinai.

Moses went up into the mountain which was covered by the cloud of God's glory for six days as the glory of the Lord rested upon it. On the seventh day God called to Moses out of the midst of the cloud, and Moses entered it and met with Him. [Exodus 24:15-16, 18a].

**There is a lesson for the Church of the Lord Jesus here:**

How many times have we been to a gathering of the saints and afterwards gone home rejoicing in the manifestation of God's presence in our midst? Perhaps we really sensed His presence and were greatly blessed, but *did we confront the Lord God **Himself**?* I believe Moses' experience teaches us that we can be in the presence of God and yet not experience God personally!

Remember that Moses waited six days near the cloud which manifested God's glory, yet did not encounter the Lord God Himself personally until the seventh day when God spoke to him. And after meeting with the Lord, Moses' face shone — it radiated with God's glory. [Exodus 34:29]. However, because of his being so near such a manifestation of God's Presence and glory, perhaps Moses' face would have been affected in a similar way had he come down from the mount after only six days, *before* he met face to face with the Lord.

### God's Ultimate Call To Us:

We need to stay ever aware of God's ultimate call to us — relationship with Himself; union and communion with the Living God. It is a travesty to the Spirit of God for us to gather together to speak and sing to and of the Lord, only to go home satisfied without ever really encountering God Himself.

### How awesome this is!

Mark 5:24-34 contains the story of the woman with an issue of blood. She pressed through the crowd that she might just touch the hem of Jesus' garment and draw from Him the power to bring health to her diseased body.

When she did finally make it to Him and touched His clothes, she was instantly healed. Then Jesus, perceiving that power had gone out from Himself, began inquiring as to who had touched Him.

His disciples could hardly believe what they were hearing! What could He mean by wanting to know who touched Him when so many people were pressing upon Him???

### Ah, but here we see the lesson:

Though many were in His presence, only one truly encountered Him intimately and with at least a partial revelation of Who He was and still is. [Hebrews 13:8]. Though many were "touching" Him, per se, they were not doing so with their spirit — in faith.

### Are we as one of the pressing multitudes,

ever near Him but never really experiencing the inflow of His life and power? Or are we as the one who, despite the experience of the masses, pressed on to experience the reality of His power and to draw upon His divinity in faith, knowing that He is the able source of supply to meet all of our needs?

It is a certainty that those who have given themselves unreservedly to the Lord are never alone. The Lord's Presence is always with them, for they are in Him and He is in them. [Colossians 2:7, 10; Ephesians 2:21-22; John 15:4; Colossians 1:27]. He has promised to never leave nor forsake those that belong to Him. [Deuteronomy 31:6, 8; Hebrews 13:5].

**However, it is just as true**

that there is a wonderful, unique life of intimacy and union with the Lord that is reserved for those that truly love Him, walking in obedience to Him in all things. [Psalm 25:14; John 14:21, 23]. Note that John 14:21 and 23 are speaking of someone who loves the Lord, not a repentant sinner, because a sinner does not keep the Lord Jesus' commandments. In these verses Jesus promises a relationship of intimacy with Himself and His Father that only the faithful and obedient will ever know.

Continuing, let us again consider Moses and notice one of the points of his Sinai encounter with the Most High:

**Moses waited before the Lord.**

There was no carnal impatience and selfishness that gave God only a token acknowledgement; no halfhearted commitment that caused Moses to congratulate himself for giving some of his precious time to God. No, Moses knew that all of his time was God's because Moses was completely consecrated in his heart to the Lord.

Also, because Moses truly believed in God, He was not satisfied with anything but meeting with God Himself. He did not try to be satisfied with merely talking about the Lord or even receiving a manifestation of God's presence. No, Moses wanted God and God he got, *because God got all of Moses.*

**Conditions For Intimacy With The Lord:**

If we give ourselves to God, He will give Himself to us. If we treat Him as a Person Who can be known intimately, then intimately He will reveal Himself. On the other hand, if we treat God as some distant, unknowable figure, He will seem distant and detached from our lives.

Both in our gatherings together and in our own individual lives, let us not settle for anything less than God Himself.

God can be known!

Therefore, we must not settle for anything less, not even His blessings, gifts, and manifestations of His presence.

*God alone!*

# 17.

# The Secret of the Secret Place

**"He who dwells in the secret place** of the Most High shall abide under the shadow of the Almighty," says Psalm 91:1. How beautiful this verse has become to many of us; how comforting! Indeed, the whole 91st Psalm has become a wonderful encouragement to a number of saints, and the topic of many a message. Within this psalm are many promises of the Lord's protection, and saints for centuries have found strength and solace in the Lord as they have absorbed its message.

But just what is this secret place that most of us speak of so readily? And not only that, but how can we see the promises of this psalm become a reality in our lives; a part of our experience?

As with all of God's dealings with us, whether they be easy or difficult, His intent is to bring us into more intimate fellowship with Himself through His Spirit and His Son. None of God's dealings are an end in themselves — they all lead to Him.

Hence we see and must realize that the secret place is not just some special place of spiritual maturity that we attain to by mortification of the flesh, self-denial, or by doing some noble deed or by speaking some lofty sermon. It is not some "spooky," otherworldly state of being that detaches us from the reality of our everyday life and responsibilities — some kind of so called "Christian Nirvana" of sorts. Nor is it some physical location or mental focus.

On the contrary, the secret place speaks of the intimate union and communion we are called to walk in and live in with the Lord God Himself. It is that private, intimate relationship all of God's people are called upon to experience and in which we are to abide. From this secret place of love for and union with God, all of our life is to be lived. Yes, we are to live in this secret place — this protected, cherished, "bubble of love" — with and in our God.

"But how are we to experience this marvelous life of protection and fellowship with the Lord?" someone may ask.

### It is simple.

So simple, in fact, that many, yes, even most, completely miss it in their zealous, nearsighted and even impossible attempt to please the Lord without total dependency upon Him and maintaining intimacy with Him.

In verse 14 is found the simple yet profound answer, the secret of the secret place:

"Because he has set his love on Me, therefore will I deliver him; I will set him on high, because he knows, understands, and acknowledges My name..." [Amplified].

Hallelujah! This setting our love on Him and coming to know Him is the secret of the secret place, the secret of life, the secret of eternal life!

Remember Jesus' words to the Father, recorded in John 17:3: "And this is eternal life: that they may know You, the only true and real God, and Jesus Christ, Whom You have sent." [From AMP and NIV].

And do you recall when the Jews asked Jesus what they must do to carry out what God required? Notice the Lord Jesus' response:

"Jesus replied, 'This is the work (service) that God asks of you, that you believe in the One Whom He has sent — that you cleave to, trust, rely on and have faith in His Messenger.'" [John 6:28-29; Amplified].

They were (and so are we) to focus on Jesus — God's Messenger; not simply the words of His message!

As a matter of fact that was (and *is)*

**"The Message":**

**"Cleave to the Lord Jesus alone and steadfastly."**
That is the only way to have and give life.

All of this is speaking of relationship with the Lord; settling for nothing less than the Godhead — the Father, Son, and Holy Spirit — as the fulfillment of all of our needs and desires.

As we set our affections on things above — not on the earth; as we cause our whole focus and intent in life to be set on Jesus Christ, we will surely come to know the Father, please the Holy Spirit, glorify and reveal the Son, and thus always "abide under the shadow of the Almighty."

**To know Him is life!**

To love Him is liberty. To obey Him is joy. To know, love, and obey Him is the purpose of our existence — the reason we were born, and is *the secret of the secret place!*

# 18.

# The Call And Cost Of The Secret Place

**As we abide in Jesus** — loving Him, obeying Him, and coming to know Him — we are brought to the realization that while we have a constant and ready cleansing available for our sin, we certainly don't have to sin, and indeed we should not. [1 John 2:1]. Few people will accept this truth, just as few people ever abide in Jesus.

Oh, what a perfect inner peace is available to the children of God! If we would but perceive and pursue the Kingdom of God, and always walk in obedience to His ways, we would constantly experience the exchanging of our weaknesses for His strength, our lack for His plenty, and our fretful strivings for His confident and peaceful rest.

But most are not willing to make their calling and election sure. They are not willing to deny themselves the fleeting pleasures of sin or ego-stroking. Since they refuse to be the enemy of all that is the enemy of God, they will not take up their cross and follow Jesus. They may look at the cross with fond or melancholy feelings, but are not willing to let the cross do its intended work.

**On the cross we are to die!**

Each of us has a unique cross, but identical in one major point: It is an instrument of death where we cease from our own labors to be resurrected anew to walk in His resurrection power and carry out His labors in His Spirit.

[See Matthew 16:24-25; Mark 8:34-35; 10:21 (NKJV); and Luke 9:23-24].

It's time our cross became a real experience in our life, instead of being only an ornament we wear on a chain, a pin on a lapel, or a bumper sticker on our car!

**Jesus said,**

"If any person wills to come after Me, let him deny Himself, take up His cross daily, and follow Me." [Luke 9:23; based on Amplified Version]. If He had expressed this thinking in today's lingo, He probably would have said something like, "If anyone desires to be My disciple, he must deny his own self-made pursuits, sit in his electric chair everyday, and allow it to be plugged in."

You see, in the day that Jesus referred to taking up your cross, His hearers knew that He was referring to a means of execution that was ruthless and thorough. Likewise, the mindset and inclination of the flesh must be dealt with ruthlessly and thoroughly — we must die to our own urges and pursuits.

Only as we are faithful to say "No!" to the flesh and "Yes!" to the Lord will we ever find the fullness of His power and peace flooding in and through us. Only as we "struggle not to struggle" [See Hebrews 4:11] and determine to stay submitted only to the Lord instead of ourselves will we ever come to experience that to which He has called us.

**And to what have we been called?**

We have been called by the Lord to His rest — "the rest of God." [Hebrews 3:7-19; 4:1-11].

Our strivings cease, all fretting is released, as we come to and abide in Him, allowing Him to work His good pleasure in and through us. To young and old, newborn babe or mature follower of Christ, the call is given; the way is opened. Intimacy with our Father awaits us if we will but follow the Son in complete obedience.

If we "let go" of our ego, we may "lay hold" of Him, touching and thrilling His heart, and enjoying Him forever!

## The Secret Place (a poem)

*There is a place where few have been*
*He who abides there does not sin*
*It is a place of constant rest*
*That we enter through faith and obedience...*

*The secret place of the Most High*
                    *is*
*Prepared for those who are willing to die*
*To self, sin, — all unrighteousness*
*And who'll take up their crosses*
*And follow Him.*

*So if you're weary on the road you trod*
*Stop striving but to enter the rest of God.*
*It need not be a lifelong quest*
*To rest Your head upon His breast.*

# 19.

# Wonder of Wonders

**Most of us have heard about** "the wonders of the world." But by far, the deepest of all depths, the greatest of all knowledge, the most awesome and wonderful wonder of wonders in all of creation is the unique calling of mankind from their Creator to know Him intimately and to be united with Him — joined to Him. Far more than mere "head knowledge," this knowledge of God of which we speak is of the heart (which in turn does affect the head!). It cannot be given to us by another — we have to experience Him for ourselves. This gift of gifts of relationship with the Living God and His Son Jesus Christ, this "knowing," is what eternal life really is: the intimate knowledge of the True and Living God and Jesus Christ in a never-ending relationship. [John 17:3].

**Just think!**

God has chosen to redeem and lift up those who are willing, from one of the lowest levels of His fallen creation, to sit with Himself. From there they are to participate in governing the universe, and enjoy incomprehensible fellowship with the Most High forever.

Jesus Christ, by the Holy Spirit of God, comes to dwell within the spirit, the "heart," of any of us who accept His sacrifice and subsequent resurrection for ourselves. His personality — His Person — then actually enters into and unites with us, enabling us to live a life of unfailing purity; above all the snares of the world, the flesh, and the devil. And as we continue to offer ourselves to Him, walking in obedience to Him and His Truth, the Lord by His indwelling Spirit continues to transform us, increasing our awareness of and ability to reveal His Person and kingdom. All this He does because of "His undeserved merit and power" (that is, His "grace") that He gives to all of those who stay joined to Him and who also continue to draw their life from Him.

### Our Constant Pursuit:

Through the challenges of the circumstances of everyday life, He is teaching us to trust Him and yield in total obedience to Him in all things; not seeking our own pursuits and pleasures. He desires for us to be constantly pursuing Him and His kingdom, always moving in His perfect will.

When we are united with Jesus Christ, His Spirit increases both wisdom and the love of God within us. Also, as we draw our resources from Him, looking to Him as our only source, we are continually cleansed by His blood from the contaminating influence and control of "sin," which is "the missing of God's best;" "rebellion against God in any form."

### Our Need Of Jesus:

How desperately we need Jesus! We must trust Him explicitly, resting in Him, for He has become (for those of us that love and follow Him) our very Life.

Just as a branch cannot bear fruit apart from the vine, neither can we reveal God's character and become what He's called us to be apart from union with Jesus Christ. [John 15:1-8]. We must keep our hearts, with their love and pursuit, set continually upon Him, pursuing His will with all the discipline and tenacity of a champion runner. [1 Corinthians 9:24-27; 2 Timothy 2:4-7]. And as we continue to look to Him and develop intimate relationship with Him personally, through His Word, and in fellowship with His people, we are changed to become just like Him.

*What we love we behold, and what we behold we become like.*

**How amazing and truly wonderful is this awesome plan of God!**

What a wonder it is that the Living God should send His

beloved Son in a physical body, so that by the sacrifice and resurrection of His life and body He might redeem lost humanity. And what a wonder that God would freely give us the gift of living forever with Him by accepting as a gift what He offers us in Jesus Christ. And what an awesome wonder it is that the Living God and His Son come to live within those who follow Jesus with all of their heart!

For Jesus has said "...If a person (really) loves Me, he will keep My word — obey My teaching; and My Father will love him, and We will come to him and make our home (abode, special dwelling place) with him." [John 14:23; Amplified]. And what does He mean by these words: "...We will make our home *with* him?" He means that He and His Father will dwell within this person's physical body, just as the person does. He desires that our bodies be the "earthen vessels" that house the Divine Treasure — the Spirit of God. [See 2 Corinthians 4:7].

Therefore, those that belong to the Lord God should honor one another as the cleansed, chosen habitat of the Holy One. [Also see Chapter 33: "Knowing Others— Knowing God"].

**The Lord's Presence in *us* consecrates the ground upon which we stand; not the other way around!**

Yes, what love and tenderness we as the Lord's people would be expressing towards one another if we truly regarded each other as "sacred," "holy," "the house of God," "the sanctuary," "the Church," and other such perceptions that have been wrongly attributed to buildings made by men and to various places around the world. For if we are one of His people, then *we* are the temple, *we* are His house, and *we* are the Church; *not* a building made by man.

*God is to be glorified in His saints; not in buildings built or used by them or in certain pieces of real estate!*

The Living God has chosen not to dwell in structures that men build, regardless of the expense and expertise involved in their construction. Rather, He has chosen to dwell in a temple of His own making — the reborn human heart, veiled in a vessel (yes, clothed in a garment) of flesh, and from there enable us to perceive and pursue His unseen kingdom and work out the salvation He puts within.

Furthermore, those who belong to God have become parts of the very body of Christ. How incomprehensible the fullness of this is!

As He continues to bring us into constant and instant obedience, He will be able to fully express Himself in and through us. Just as we desire for our bodies to be responsive to our decisions, vehicles in and through which we are known and expressed, so does Jesus Christ desire a responsive, strong, healthy and well-trained body in and through which He can reveal and express Himself.

**However, the body of Christ has been plagued by its own willfulness...**

A body that doesn't respond to its head as it should is said to be "spastic" or otherwise "diseased." A cell that is bent on satisfying its own lusts and cravings is cancerous, destructive, and potentially deadly. As the Head of His body, Jesus Christ expects instant and constant responsiveness and co-operation from each of us who are the individual parts or members of it. He will most definitely have a healthy body that in no way impedes Him. All of us who are His people play a critical role in the functioning and readiness of this body for His use. Let's not ever hinder Him from being able to fully utilize it and express Himself as He sees fit.

This joining of God with man, this intimacy with and subsequent revealing of God by those of us who are willing and persistent, this highest calling of all in Jesus Christ is certainly the *"wonder of wonders!"*

**Wonder of Wonders** (a song)

*Wonder of wonders — Christ within.*
*Wonder of wonders — to be freed from all sin.*

*From glory to glory and faith to faith,*
*We're growing in Jesus by His grace.*

(chorus)*Wonder of wonders is the Lord Jesus Christ —*
*God's mystic secret; our very life.*
*He reveals Himself to, then within,*
*then through those who answer His call.*
*Yes, the Wonder of wonders is Jesus –*
*the Lord of all!*

*Learning to trust Him, yes, we're learning to yield.*
*We're learning to move only in His perfect will.*
*We're growing in wisdom and in the love of God.*
*Abiding in Jesus, we are cleansed by His blood.*

*Resting in Jesus, for He is our life.*
*We are the branches, and He is the Vine.*
*We're gazing unto Him as we run the race.*
*We're changed into His image, beholding His face.*

(chorus)*Wonder of wonders is the Lord Jesus Christ —*
*God's mystic secret; our very life.*
*He reveals Himself to, then within,*
*then through those who answer His call.*
*Yes, the Wonder of wonders is Jesus —*
*the Lord of all!*

## 20.

# Walking in the Wilderness

**What an awesome sight it was** — an entire nation following the Living God through an uncharted wilderness! By reading Exodus 13:21 and 22, and also Numbers 9:15-21, we learn that the Lord would go before the Israelites in a pillar of cloud by day and in a pillar of fire at night during their wilderness journey.

The pillar of cloud was a covering by day. In the evening the pillar of fire gave light and lit up their path. Therefore, the people could travel by night as well as day. [Psalm 105:39; Exodus 13:21].

They would move only when the cloud or fiery pillar would move. In other words, they followed the Lord, not their own desires and plans, and would travel or remain encamped and stationary, sometimes for more than a month, at the command of the Lord alone. [Numbers 9:21-23].

**There is quite a lesson here for us.**

In 1 Corinthians 10:11 we are told that the experiences of the Israelites in their wilderness journey happened to them as examples and were written down as warnings for us — we on whom the ends of the ages have come.

The wilderness was a land of deserts, pits, drought, the shadow of death, and deep darkness. It was a land that no man had passed through and where no man dwelt. [Jeremiah 2:6].

Yet this difficult path was the Lord's choice to take His people to the land of promise and plenty. However, even though the circumstances were so extremely trying and potentially hazardous, the Lord completely guarded and watched over them: going before them [Exodus 13:21], following them [1 Corinthians 10:4], and walking in their midst! [Deuteronomy 23:14].

Here in the harsh, deadly wilderness, the vast and dreadful desert, a thirsty and waterless land with venomous snakes and scorpions, the people of God were supposed to learn to rely totally on the Lord alone for strength and survival. Here they were to learn to trust in and drink from the spiritual Rock that followed them, which was Christ. [Deuteronomy 8:15 and 1 Corinthians 10:4].

### As with the Israelites of old, so with us:

Similar to them, we find ourselves engaged in a journey in the spiritual realm that is an impossible task for people on their own to endure or even conceive. We, like these Israelites, must move at God's direction and bidding, "following the cloud," so to speak. Otherwise, we may find ourselves going "round 'n' round" a so called "holy mountain" of our experience which was holy only because He was once there! In the meantime, the Lord may be long gone, leading the faithful few who love Him and trust in Him to the point of being devoted to Him alone.

Regardless of the greatness of revelation or manifestation of God's presence in any particular wilderness location, that "haven of rest and blessing" becomes a place of barrenness once the Lord moves on. It is only the Lord's Presence that makes holy any location or experience, and His absence means certain turmoil and distress — perhaps even death.

*Any place in the wilderness that was safe and secure was only that way when the Lord was there...*

Our mount of transfiguration experience or Sinai experience could spell our doom, becoming our undoing, if we cling to these instead of constantly clinging to the Lord. When once the Lord has moved on, you can put "Ichabod" over the door of any situation or experience. "Ichabod" means "Alas, the Glory!," and belongs to a category of names expressing mourning for an absent deity. [Harper's

Bible Dictionary].

So we see our obedience to the Lord is an absolute necessity upon which our very survival depends — especially in these last days!

Furthermore, not only is our journey full of dangers to both the inner and outer man, but also, yesterday's heavenly provision will not suffice for today's needs...

## The Lesson Of The Manna:

In Exodus 16:19-20 we read of Moses telling the people to not save the daily gatherings of manna till morning. Those that did not obey found that the manna bred worms and stank.

The manna was a heavenly provision, a breadlike substance given by God to the children of Israel to provide strength and life. Jesus referred to Himself as the ultimate heavenly provision, the "Heavenly Bread," whose body was offered as a sacrifice for the life of the world. [John 6:48-51]. The lesson of the manna is that we must daily maintain our communion with and "feeding upon" Jesus as the Bread of Life.

Yesterday's provision was for yesterday. Today must have its own!

## What am I getting at?

Simply that our love and passion must be for the Lord alone. Nothing must be allowed to take the place of our earnest and radical devotion to His Person. This includes all experiences, all revelations of His will and Word, and any wonderful memories we may hold dear, regardless of how much "of God" they may have been.

Remember, as we have discovered in a previous chapter ["Do We Know The Scriptures *And* The Word Of God?"], even the Bible, God's ultimate tool outside of His Own Person by which He reveals Himself and instructs us, is not to be substituted for a personal and intimate relationship with the Son of God. [John 5:39-40]. As a matter of fact, in these verses Jesus points out that the Scriptures, apart from Him, do not even offer life!

Are the Scriptures a tool? Yes! The Craftsman? No! Instruction? Yes! The Instructor? No!

## How desperately we must stay in vital contact and union with the Lord!

Like the pillar of fire by night, He leads and warms us, and like the pillar of cloud by day, He protects us from the searing heat and fierce winds. He is our only means of survival in this uncharted, deadly course through the natural as well as the spiritual realm of "snakes" (a symbol of our enemy — Satan, and his demons).

The Lord Jesus alone is able to lead His new creation nation through the wilderness of testing and revelation to its destiny.

He even makes the barren wilderness a place of joy and supernatural revelation and provision. [Isaiah 43:19]. His blessed Presence comforts us and makes even a deplorable and deadly situation an oasis of delight and joy!

## We must keep our focus entirely on the Lord.

We mustn't become enamored and caught up even in His times of refreshing or His seasons of rest and revelation. When He with the cloud of His anointing moves, we must move with Him, moment to moment maintaining our gaze and focus on Him, knowing that our life is from *Him*; not from His means of ministering to us. Without Him, our times and experiences of light and life will be turned into darkness and death.

## However, we need not die in the wilderness,

nor even fear it. If we will but keep our focus and our mental pursuit on and for Him alone, we will always walk in His victory and peace. [2 Corinthians 2:14; Isaiah 26:3-4].

Therefore, walking in His salvation — free from defeat and full of the glory of the revelation of Himself — let us always love and follow the Lord of the pillar of cloud and fire!

# 21.

# Our "Here 'n' Now" Response Determines Our "By 'n' By" Reward

**Jesus said** that He would come to and would reveal Himself to those who obey Him. [John 14:21].

Since love is the fulfillment of the law [Romans 13:8-10], and to bear one another's burdens is to fulfill the Law of Christ [Galatians 6:2], we see that one prerequisite of the revelation of Jesus Christ to a believer is their willingness to serve the Lord's people, helping them through hard times. Thereby do they fulfill their role as a brother or sister: born for adversity — born to come to the assistance of others in need. [Proverbs 17:17].

This thought is also reflected in Jeremiah 22:15, where the Lord points out that a certain king's upright living and good deeds, defending the cause of the poor and needy, was the essence of knowing Him. From these Scriptures, we see evidenced a principle of God:

*Our relationship with the natural, temporal realm determines our relationship with the spiritual, eternal realm.*

Jesus taught that if someone is not faithful and trustworthy in the handling of worldly wealth — wealth that can be seen — that person would not be entrusted with the true, spiritual, unseen treasures of the Kingdom of God. [Luke 16:11].

We can easily make the mistake of thinking that our present circumstances here on earth are not really important. We may even feel that they are holding us back from realizing our true potential and calling in God. However, on the contrary, God will not increase our place in His kingdom until we deal responsibly and in a manner upright and pleasing to Him with worldly, temporal things.

### Knowing God is more "earthy" than most people think.

For the majority of people, it rarely includes "spooky," otherworldly experiences.

### As an example, consider Abraham...

Though when we read about him in Scripture it may seem that he was often having visions and dreams of God, in reality some of these experiences were years apart! What happened in the meantime? The day in, day out events of everyday life.

Of course, God didn't forsake His servant during those seasons of the seemingly mundane. Nevertheless, we can see in Abraham's experience that supernatural manifestations of God were the exception, not the rule.

But do bear in mind what we have been discussing:

This is not something bad — this is the general plan of God!

God doesn't want our attention and focus to be placed upon supernatural, "otherworldly" experiences. Instead, He wants us to set our hearts and minds on Him, by a continual choice. *This* constitutes the test of the present life — living in the midst of the ordinary and mundane, yet living for and looking to the supernatural, unseen world of the spiritual domain of God.

### The test Of life: The essence of real faith —

living *in* one realm while living *for* another.

It is the Lord's will to reveal Himself and His eternal attributes and kingdom in the midst of this fallen, stubborn world.

This insight causes us to look upon the events of everyday life in a new, exciting way. No longer seen as impediments to us becoming what God desires us to be, we begin

to elevate everyday situations to their proper place: opportunities in which, because of our responding to and looking
to an invisible God, He can reveal Himself to a lost world,
and draw it back to Himself.

### Therefore, rejoice!

This knowing God is more than ritual and form, and is
more than a "bolt out of the sky" experience. No, it's an
ever continuing walk with the Lord that requires getting
involved with others where they are that we might help to
lift them to where they ought to be [1 Corinthians 9:19-22;
Jude 22-23], always aware that at this present time the
unseen realm is intricately tied and related to the present
world and its circumstances.

### So lift the mundane into the eternal.

Rejoice and be faithful in the little things, for the one
that is faithful with little (the present world and its daily
demands) will be faithful and entrusted with much (the
eternal, hidden riches of the intimate knowledge of God
and His unseen kingdom)!

*Our here 'n' now response determines our by 'n' by re-
ward!*

## 22.

# Ready In Season
# And Out Of Season

**Some years ago,** I accepted a request from a pastor to "take" their evening meeting. Without specifying it, I'm sure the pastor wanted me to make sure the gathering was led of the Spirit of God in decency and in order. [1 Thessalonians 5:19-22; 1 Timothy 1:6; 1 Corinthians 14:40].

Later in the afternoon, the secretary of the fellowship called and asked, "Are you prepared?"

"Prepared for what?" I responded.

"For the meeting tonight," was her reply.

"I *live* prepared," I said, and then quickly explained that I didn't answer her in such a way to be haughty, but to just express the reality of the way God had showed me to live...

"If I have to get prepared, then where am I *now*?" I inquired.

The Lord had been teaching me to walk in the consciousness of His ever present Presence and the importance of constantly abiding in Him, maintaining alertness and ready obedience towards His Spirit. Each and every moment we are to "be ready instant in season and out of season" [From 2 Timothy 4:2; NAS] to minister and/or be up to whatever the situation may require.

Now I know that for many believers, having a "quiet time" or "devotions" each day with the Lord is an integral part of their day to day activities. I am by no means speaking against such a discipline, especially if the Spirit of the Lord is leading someone to do it. Also, there are times and seasons out of the ordinary requiring that we set aside our normal schedules and commitments to seek the Lord. And, for many, having a special time of preparation before a designated time of ministry or before a meeting is extremely important, even crucial. What I'm trying to emphasize here, however, is the absolute and utter importance of *maintaining* intimacy and right relationship with the Lord and a constant state of preparation...

*Our whole life should be consumed in yieldedness to God* — each and every moment; constantly and continually.

**Nothing, including even prayer, can substitute for a *life* of purity and total abandonment to God.**

This doesn't mean that prayer is not a part of living in purity and total abandonment to God. However, we shouldn't live a self-seeking life of carnality and then use prayer as a last-ditch effort to procure God's favor on us or for a particular situation. If we are selfish, carnal, and lazy, we are living wickedly and are more likely to receive a rebuke and discipline from the Lord rather than His favor, even if we are one of His people...

Remember Jesus' story of the talents: The Lord referred to His unprofitable servant as wicked and lazy. [Matthew 25:26; NIV]. Now take note of the following Scriptures: "The sacrifice of the wicked is an abomination to the Lord..." [Proverbs 15:8a; NAS]. "He who turns away His ear from hearing the law [of God and man], even His *prayer* is an abomination, hateful and revolting to God." [Proverbs 28:9; based on Amplified]. Yes, prayer is a wonderful blessing available to and needed by us, but let us not deceive ourselves or others — *it is not a cure-all.* Prayer (or any other activity, for that matter, such as Bible study, singing psalms, or whatever) was never intended to be a substitute for righteous living. An aid for righteous living? Yes! A substitute? No!

In short: Prayer does indeed play an important role in

our growing and developing in grace and purity, and *if we are pure, we will pray, but just because we pray does not mean that we are pure!*

The greater includes the lesser. [Also See Chapter 14].

## I have often seen people praying with great intensity and near frenzy

in supposed preparation for a meeting they were about to attend. Now I'm sure a real work of the Spirit of God has been accomplished during some of those times. Most certainly, true, Holy Spirit led intercession will often produce such manifestations.

Nevertheless, much of the straining and effort in prayer that is put forth can sometimes be an indication of a state of spiritual decline or apathy. I mean, if we have to make such an effort to get ready for a meeting, then where are we before we begin such a preparation??? I do thank God for the earnestness that is probably very sincere at such times, and if a person is really in need of preparation, then by all means they should engage in it! However, I believe the highest way is for us to *abide* and *walk* in readiness, and not have to suddenly alter our course or present state of being to fulfill what God is requiring of us.

## Most definitely,

frenzied and harried praying should never take the place of maintaining through faith and obedience a perpetual state of submission to God and spiritual fitness so that we are always instantly ready and available to totally fulfill God's will at any given moment.

Are *we* **ready** at all times, maintaining a right relationship and intimacy with the Lord Jesus that enables us to be ever useful and fruitful in His kingdom? Are *we* **ready** *"in season and out of season"*?

We *can* be...

# 23.

# Present Yourselves Unto Him

**If we will offer ourselves completely** and unreservedly to the Lord, we will find Him to be our constant, reliable source of victory. Regardless of the many trials and battles we will face, we shall find that he will not let even one hair of our heads perish, because He loves us so.

Rather than demanding the fulfilling of a set of rules and rituals to please Him, the Lord instead requires a heart that is willing to follow Him, hungry for Him and His Truth, and obedient to His every desire. A heart that is offered completely to Him, such as this, He will fill by His Spirit with His love and power.

We must not allow our hearts to be anxious or afraid. We can comfort ourselves in the knowledge that He said He would never leave us, and by His power, with Jesus' name on our lips, all the demons that exist will turn and flee from us in terror.

**Sing to the Lord Jesus songs of praise!**

He is our very life and the dock that secures us in any and all storms. He is always faithful, the Lord of all, and by His love and power He watches over us and protects us, saving us from ourselves, our enemy Satan, and the snares of this present life. His Presence also enables us to remain calm and serene, regardless of the circumstances in which we may find ourselves.

Many in the world brag of foolish pursuits and vain accomplishments, but let us always and only brag about and boast in and of the Lord Jesus. He is the only One worthy of our praise.

**And just think!**

When we see Him as He is, we shall be changed and be just like Him.

In view of God's greatness and mercy, we must never give in for even a moment to any of the devil's lies and temptations. He only desires to separate us from the Lord Jesus. It is Jesus who really loves us and has every right to demand everything of us because He bought us from sin and Satan with His very own blood.

It is a fact that the earth will be severely punished for its rebellion against God, but those that remain in union with the Lord Jesus will find God's help, strength, and undeserved favor saving them from God's soon coming wrath.

Let us all worship and devote ourselves completely to the Lord Jesus.

Though He was God, He took on and tabernacled in human flesh. He fully paid the price for our crimes against His divine decrees by dying on the hill called "Calvary."

**Yet look!**

As He said would happen, He was raised to life again by His Father's power and was given such glory and honor that it is beyond human capacity to conceive, let alone tell! And now the Lord Jesus is the undisputed conqueror of death, the grave, and Hell!

*Nothing,* therefore, must be allowed to hold us back from persistently pursuing that for which God called us. His intent for His dealings with us is for them to bring us to a deeper and greater confrontation and union with the Lord Jesus.

Also, God's immeasurable love is to be the very atmosphere in which we constantly live.

**Think upon this fact:**

When we were sinners, separated from God, He willed the death of His Son to secure our release from sin and its just condemnation. Yet now that we are His, the unre-

stricted power of His resurrection life is offered to those of
us who choose to be totally His.

Look at the power and greatness of God's gift for sinners!

How much greater is the untapped power and greatness
of His resurrection life that is available to His children!
[Romans 5:10].


**Present Yourselves Unto Him** (a poem)

*Present yourselves unto Him.*
*Let Him have His way.*
*He will be your Victory —*
*He will be your Stay.*
*Though the storms of trials beset you on many a hand,*
*He will let not one hair perish on your beloved head.*

*Give unto the Master all that He requires —*
*a willing, hungry, obedient heart*
*that He can fill with His love and power.*
*Let not your heart be troubled —*
*He said He'd never leave,*
*and all the hosts of darkness*
*must before you turn and flee.*

*Sing praises to our Jesus!*
*Our Life and Rock is He;*
*our Faithful Lord and Keeper,*
*and Calm Serenity.*
*Though many boast of folly,*
*surely He our Boast shall be.*
*And we shall be just like Him*
*when His precious face we see.*

*So yield not to the devil*
*who seeks to part you from the One*
*Who truly loves and helps you*

*and bought you for His own.*
*Though the earth shall stagger*
*'neath the blows of our God's wrath —*
*Safely hid in our Lord Jesus,*
*we'll not of our God's grace lack.*

*Worship and adore the mighty God of victory*
*Who secured our pardon fully by dying on Calvary.*
*Raised to splendor glorious*
*beyond what human tongue can tell*
*The Lord Jesus reigns as victor*
*over death, the grave, and Hell!*

*Press on then for the mark*
*to which He's calling us in His Son,*
*for our Father longs to see us lost —*
*within His boundless love.*
*The **death** of Jesus Christ His Son*
*for sinners did atone,*
*but His resurrection **life** is given*
*to those who yield their all.*

## 24.

# Saying "YES!" Means Saying "NO!"

**Little Johnny was eager to go out and play.**

"Now don't go into or across the street, Johnny," his mother said.

"O.K., Mom," he said, as he rushed out the door.

After enjoying playing in his yard for awhile, some of his friends across the street began to call to him...

"Johnny, come on over. Bill's got some new toys, and man, you just gotta see 'em!"

"No, my mom said I have to stay out of the street, so I can't come over."

"Aw, come on, Johnny! It ain't gonna hurt nothin' !"

"Listen," Johnny said, "I said 'Yes!' to her, so that means I have to say 'No!' to you!"

Little Johnny was seeing something that many believers miss: Submission to authority is more than a confession or statement of intention. True submission consists of obedience.

Furthermore, the proof and evidence of our submission to God occurs only as we face an option to His will.

Then, if we are truly yielded to God, we will confirm our allegiance by corresponding actions. We must turn from, resist and say "No!" to the opposing, disobedient option, and we must aggressively turn towards God and obey Him. Saying "Yes!" to God means saying "No!" to anything contrary to Him.

**For a number of years,**

I was under a persuasion (notice the wording: "under")

that if I offered myself to God, consciously chose His will, and yielded to Him by an act of my will during prayer, then any desire that occurred while I maintained this attitude of submission must be from Him. As I felt a desire to do something, I would immediately yield it to God, and if He didn't want me to do it, I would get a "check" in my spirit, otherwise I would proceed with my desire.

## I thought I had found the secret to really walking with God:

Simply yield yourself to Him constantly and He will lead you through your desires and inner "checks."

For a while this worked beautifully, and God led me this way. The time came, however, when He stopped speaking inwardly to me on every issue.

The confusion that ensued almost drove me nuts!

Suddenly, I found myself desiring fleshly things, and God wasn't inwardly "checking" me! I was barraged with many thoughts:

"Does God want me to give in and do these things?"

"Has He forsaken me?"

"Maybe He is testing me: Perhaps He will let me *begin* to do these things, *then* He will check me."

"Perhaps He wants me to enter a scene of temptation so I can witness about Him!"

## "The Dilemma":

Such thinking may seem ludicrous, but when you've lived your life for so long in a certain way that you were convinced was right, it can be most disconcerting when things seem to be changing. Yes, I found myself in what I termed "The Dilemma": "Yielding to God in prayer, I nevertheless continued to have strong fleshly attractions."

How distraught I was! How torn!

After suffering in this way in some form or fashion for a number of years, I began to perceive the Truth. God had been very gracious and had protected me to a great extent from my lack of understanding for quite some time. He had controlled my every situation — telling me where to go, when to go, when to move, when to be still, when and what to speak, and so forth.

How wonderful it seemed! How innocent it was! And because of that very point — innocence — God had to change His way of dealing with me...

Innocence is grand for awhile, but approved and mature character is developed only by moral tests and choices.

The Lord was now wanting *me* to make good, righteous decisions — based upon the way He had been leading me.

The infant stage had come to an end. It was time to grow up.

### To further illustrate:

For a while in a child's life, especially during infancy, everything in its environment is controlled — where the child lays, where the child plays, the toys that surround it, and so forth. Until the child has been taught some realities of life, such as the wisdom of not playing in the street, his or her options are limited, and the concerned and aware parent will restrict the child's personal choices, perhaps letting the child play only in the back yard, for instance.

But the time comes, hopefully, when the child, having been taught by the parent and having proven a level of maturity, responsibility, and respect for the parent, will be allowed to choose whether he or she desires to play in the back or the front yard. The child can now be trusted by the parent not to run into the street, and so the parent gives the child greater liberty.

### Such is the way of our Father and His kingdom.

I began to realize that His apparent silence was actually an honor for me, because He was in effect saying that it was time I grew up and made some decisions on my own — based on His past dealings and instructions.

Would I prove to be a vessel suitable for the Master's use by separating myself from evil and its influences? [2 Timothy 2:19-21]. Was I going to make my calling and election sure? [2 Peter 1:10]. Was I going to follow Peter's admonition to "add to" that which God had begun? [2 Peter

1:5-7]. Was I going to heed the grace of God which has appeared to all of us, bringing salvation and teaching us to say "No!" to all ungodliness? [Titus 2:11-14].

So I began to see that I have a part in this process of maturing. My saying "Yes!" to God must include a resounding "No!" to any contrary desire.

## Consider our Lord Jesus.

Even He was faced with this dilemma...

We know that He was always submitted to His Father and was always desirous to see His Father's will accomplished. Nevertheless, in the Garden of Gethsemane, on the night of His betrayal, He agonized to the shedding of blood in His struggle against sin! [Luke 22:44 and Hebrews 12:4]. He prayed, not once, but three times, to be delivered if at all possible from the terrible ordeal of drinking to the last drop from the cup of God's wrath. [Matthew 26:36-43].

Simply put, the Father had a plan, and frankly, Jesus did not readily want to do it. His flesh and mind screamed against the terror of what was upon Him.

But Hallelujah! Though His flesh was weak, His spirit was willing.

Jesus faced a choice of whether to fully accomplish God's will or to give in to His own desires, and though He was honest in facing and admitting His apprehension, He, nevertheless, resolutely chose God's will over His own. His submission was made complete. Remember our Master's words: "O My Father, if it be possible, let this cup pass from me. Nevertheless, not what I desire, but what you desire." [See Matthew 26:39-43].

Also, John 5:30, 6:38, and Romans 15:3 are other Scriptures that reveal that the Lord Jesus chose His Father's will — not His own: "...I seek not to please Myself, but I seek to please Him Who sent Me." [John 5:30c; based on NIV].

"For I have come down from Heaven not to do My will but to do the will of Him Who sent Me." [John 6:38; based on NIV].

"For even Christ did not please Himself..." [Romans 15:3a; based on NIV].

**Similarly, we constantly must choose**

whether to follow God or yield to our fleshly desires. By the indwelling of His Spirit, we who have given ourselves to Him and received the gift of salvation have received the power to conquer every haughty, carnal, and damning option to God's will. We have been empowered to fully accomplish the will of God and lay hold of the prize of His calling and the eternal life to which we have been summoned.

We must choose, as did the Son of God, to say "Yes!" to God and "No!" to contrary desires. They both go hand in hand. One is not complete without the other. This we must do if we truly desire to fully experience the Lord's victory and enablement to totally accomplish God's will.

*Saying "YES!" means saying "NO!"*

# 25.

# From Faith *Towards* God To Union *With* God

**Hebrews 6:1-3** encourages us to go on to perfection, not laying again the elementary principles of the doctrine of Christ. One of these first, "elementary" principles mentioned is instruction regarding "faith towards God." The passage then goes on to say that we will go on from these elemental principles if God permits.

Well, believe me, God is permitting!

He longs to see us grow in the knowledge of Himself and His Son, becoming strong as we draw all our strength from His Spirit unceasingly.

One thing that I've seen through these verses is that, while we never cease from putting our faith in Him alone, we are to grow beyond simply having "faith towards God." We mature *in* Him; not just *towards* Him.

[Again, this is certainly not implying that we ever come to a place where our faith is in something or someone other than Him alone. No, not by any means!].

You see, one of the wonders of "Immanuel" ("God with us") and His indwelling Spirit is this truth: Christ *in* us is our hope of Glory. [Colossians 1:27]. Many times in the New Testament there are references to our being in Him and His being in us. [See John 14:20; 15:4-7; Romans 8:9-10; 1 Corinthians 6:17; 2 Corinthians 1:21; 5:17, 21; Colossians 1:27; 1 John 2:24].

**Simply put:**

Our first perception of faith *towards* God is to disappear in the wonderful and awe inspiring insight and experience of union *with* God! Then, our faith will no longer be expressed merely "towards" Someone detached, separate from us, or "out there somewhere." Rather, our faith will remain intact and stronger than ever as we experience *union* with this Mighty God in Whom we place our faith.

Recall 1 Corinthians 6:17, where we are instructed that "...the person who is united to the Lord becomes one spirit with Him." [Amplified Version]. And in Ephesians 5:30 we read that "...we are members of His body, of His flesh and of His bones." [NKJV].

**This is definitely speaking of union.**

Also, consider Ephesians 1:22-23, where we are again told that we are the body of Christ (just think — His body!), of which He is the Head. There certainly is a union between a living body and its head!

From these and other passages we see that a marvelous miracle has taken place in redemption:

God not only saves us and then merely leads or empowers us from a distance, as it were, or even just by coming to live in us. No, bless His name! He even joins Himself to us, and we with Him.

How totally awesome this is! How incredible!!

**Once, years ago,**
I was in a discussion with a pastor concerning a particular occupation that I was engaged in at the time:

"Would you want Jesus to come back while you were doing this?" He asked.

I let him know that it would be fine with me:

"He sees me *now*," I exclaimed. "He's not going to come back and 'catch me,' so to speak. He's with me *now* — *always* — and it wouldn't take Him by surprise. I don't hang Him up outside my workplace and say, 'I'll check Ya' later, Lord, after I'm off work.' **No!** He's with me always!"

We are to walk in the consciousness of His ever abiding Presence, drawing upon Him as our life at *all* times, in *every* situation.

As believers, we are in Him, and He is in us. We are

joined to Him, and He is joined to us.

*This* **is the new creation:**

The *union* of God and man!

However, hear me out carefully. This is a wonderful truth; one that should humble us greatly, instilling the fear of God in us and encouraging us to walk in holiness, good deeds, love, and power.

But listen. This truth must not be perverted, rendering it a lie and destructive...

We don't become God!

We are His people — He is our God. We are His sheep — He is the Shepherd. We are His body — but Jesus the Lord will always be the one and only Head.

He alone will have the pre-eminence. He is the First-born; the A and the Z.

We are the ones that by nature need Him. He by nature does not need us.

The only reason He needs us is because He planned and designed it to be so — He decided that He would need us to make up the members of the body of Christ and that we would have a part in the revealing of Himself to His creation. This was an act of His voluntary will, not of necessity.

The Almighty is almighty; the All-Sufficient and Self-Sufficient One! We are the privileged vessels who have received of His grace and mercy.

**How wonderful He is!**

And how privileged we are, that we should be called "the sons of God," "the new creation," joined to the Omnipotent One by a mystery of His Spirit!

As the truth of this union takes a proper role and place in our perception and life, we begin to see that if we are faithful to Him He can do such a work in us that the longings and desires that we fulfill will be His, and truly, our meat, our strength, our life will be to do His will.

**Sinning — It is possible, but not acceptable...**

This is not to say that we lose our capacity to "go our own way," that is, to "sin," for if we do not abide in Him we certainly will be in sin. But the enablement that He has provided in His Son equips us to not sin. This is His will. [Read Romans 2:4-13; 3:28; 6:1-23; 7:6; 8:3-14; 1 Peter 1:15-17; 2:1, 9, 11; 3:10-12; 2 Peter 1:2-11; Titus 2:11-15; 1 John 2:1, 4, 6; 3:2-11; 5:3-5; Jude 24-25].

For the believer in Jesus, born of God, there is no excuse for sin. Sin is an option to God's will that we *choose,* either by doing something we shouldn't, or by not doing what we know we should. [1 John 3:4; James 4:17].

**Simply put:**

*We will never stray if we always obey, and if we sin, we're not abiding in Him.*

As we follow Him, we will not only just discover and *do* His will. We will also walk in such a way as to *be* His will!

We must settle for nothing less than this: absolute conformity to His desires and plans, so that He alone may be glorified and revealed in and through us.

"Let us go on," therefore, from faith *towards* God, to walking and living in the reality of union *with* God!!

It is our heritage and His desire!

# 26

# Let It Burn

**Oh God, let your purifying fire** rid me of those things that displease you, even though it seems as though You're taking so much away. I know that the gains I shall find as I nurture our relationship will far outweigh any seeming losses. And I know that if I deny myself, truly responding as a dead man would to the allurements of this world and sin, I will find, now, genuine, eternal life that will please You and be energized by You.

**Be glorified in all this, my God.**

I know that Your dealings, though often extremely painful, will produce a triumphant life, so I ask You, even though I feel like I'm dying, to do a thorough work. Truly, when You have completed this priceless work within my inner being, I'll walk in the holiness of Jesus Christ Your Son and will be confident and triumphant in my struggle against the lust of the flesh, the lust of the eyes, and the pride of life. Your work will make of me a teachable, humble victor over sin. So bring glory to Yourself and reveal Yourself in me regardless of any resistance from a defiled ego, because my one desire is to be like Jesus Christ my Lord.

**Hush and be still, my soul and mind!**

Only by abiding in the Lord will you find rest, true peace, and contentment. I will not please God to the uttermost by giving in to restlessness and troubled, worried thoughts.

Instead, rejoice, my heart! The Lord is for you and will not forsake you. Don't even think of listening to the lie of the enemy that would suggest differently. Choose to draw close to the Lord and your inward conviction will lead to conforming, corresponding outward action.

Likewise, He has promised to draw close to you and enjoy sweet fellowship with you. If you are always yielding to and abiding in Him you will surely delight His heart. Anything less than this is unacceptable to Him.

Praise Him, O my soul! He is the foundation of your existence, your protector from all enemies, and your solid and only strength. That which the Lord has spoken will surely come to pass:

He will completely set you free from everything that holds you back and weighs you down in your pursuit of Him. Also, He will heal all your wounds and remove every dreadful, tainted trace of sin.

The only restrictions the Lord will place upon you are the restrictions of His own pure love...

**Move in His love and you may do as you wish, because:**

*If you are moving in His love, then you are moving in His will.*

Allow the One who bought you with His blood to use you like a magnet to attract and draw His fallen creation back to Himself.

Our Father is longing to enjoy sweet, intimate fellowship with us. Jesus His Son has become our very life, and only by drawing from Him can we grow to become everything Father has planned for us to be. The blessed Holy Spirit has been sent to empower and impel us to love and serve our Lord with all of our heart. Yes, the complete Godhead participates in this wonderful, evermore intimate relationship with us.

**Hear what Father — our God, our Daddy, our *Papa* — says:**

"Don't listen to doubts that would come to you. I offer you My strength, My life, My all; and only in receiving all I am and all I offer will you find total peace.

"Draw close to Me. You have My assurance that I will be with you, even in the hardest of times, to bring you through victoriously. Joined with Me you shall overcome.

"Be strong. Don't listen to thoughts of fear and defeat. To do that you would be denying the fact that I've promised to never forsake you and to always be there to see you through victoriously in all of life's struggles.

"Although you shall face times of great testing when you feel nothing and it doesn't seem as if I even exist, don't be as those who cease from following Me. This will always lead to destruction.

"Though fear would attempt to discourage you from the Light, don't give in!

"And although carnal and fleshly lusts may attempt to set your very soul on fire, know that you have My promise that I will not only be with you, but will also enable you to always overcome.

"But don't get haughty or self-sufficient, deceiving yourself. For I alone am your strength and ability to overcome enemies more powerful than you are apart from union with Me.

**"Always remember this:**

"At Calvary it was not the cry of a dying martyr, but of a totally victorious King, when Jesus pierced the blackness of a dreadful yet glorious day with the words: 'It is finished!'

"His victory is truly your victory if you will believe and accept it, and walk steadfastly with Me."

**Let It Burn** (a poem)

*Let it burn, let it burn, Oh rid me of the dross.*
*Let it burn, let it burn, though great be the loss.*
*For greater yet shall be the gain*
*that I shall find in You, O Lord...*
*and dying once I live again*

*to You, for You, by You, my God.*

*I shall live! Oh yes,*
*You said that by Your grace I'd thrive.*
*So thoroughly do it now, Lord,*
*though I feel that I shall die.*
*For when Your priceless work is done —*
*Your work within complete,*
*I'll be just like Your First-Born Son,*
*when with sin I meet.*

*For dressed in robes of righteousness*
*and calm serenity,*
*I'll fight the fight of faith as He*
*in perfect humility.*
*So glorify Yourself in me*
*though ego scream and clamor —*
*To be like Jesus Christ my Lord*
*is all that really matters.*

*Hush! My soul. Be still, my mind!*
*The Lord alone is Rest.*
*In restless moods and anxious thoughts,*
*I'll not walk in His best.*
*Rejoice, my heart! Rejoice, I say!*
*The Lord is on your side.*
*He has not cast you off, oh no!*
*Don't listen to that lie.*
*Draw close to Him*
*and He shall draw so very close to you.*
*Yield to — yes — Abide in Him;*
*nought else will ever do.*

*Praise Him, my soul! Praise Him —*
*my Rock and Shield and Strength is He!*
*He shall fulfill what He has said*
*and completely set you free...*
*from all that does encumber you*

*and weigh you down within;*
*from every earthly wound*
*and dreadful, tainted trace of sin.*

*You shall move without restraint*
*within the bounds of love,*
*and draw each creature nearer Him*
*Who bought you by His blood.*
*Father longs to have us close,*
*and in His Son we'll grow,*
*and by His Spirit we'll stay infilled —*
*our God we'll truly know.*

*So hearken not to doubts*
*though they should clamor for your mind.*
*My strength is yours, My life, My all,*
*and in Me peace you'll find.*
*Draw near to Me —*
*I shall be there in every windy gale,*
*and see you through to victory —*
*In Me you shall prevail.*

*Be strong, My son, and hearken not*
*to thoughts of woe and retreat.*
*I'll never leave, I'll never go —*
*I'll be there when you meet*
*the deadly drought, the fears, the lusts*
*that come along the way.*
*In Me you'll surely overcome.*
*Be strong in Me I say!*

*The victory is secured, My son,*
*the battle's surely won,*
*When on Me you rely alone.*
*It is finished —*
*IT IS DONE!*

# 27

# A Prayer

**Lord, I feel so weighed down** and depressed within my heart because I seem to resist Your dealings, refusing to relinquish everything I am and have to You. O God, change me, Lord, and make me sensitive and willing to immediately obey Your precious Spirit speaking to me.

Lord Jesus, You are my everything, and my very life is really You having come to live within me and to be joined to me. I desire to love You in a greater way and respond to Your command to take up my cross. I know this means that I must daily deny my own pursuits, and eagerly pursue Your desires and aims. Help me also, Lord, to fulfill Your command to cling to You desperately, always abiding in You by obeying You, knowing that without You I can do nothing of any significance before God.

Oh hear me now; change me and work in me to look to You each and every moment of my life. Continue to transform me until Your very nature, life, and love floods through me as a brilliant light for all to see, so that they might be drawn to You.

**Thank you, Lord,**
that everything I will ever need and should long for is in Jesus, and as I know Him better, His traits become mine. He in me, and I in Him: This union conforms me to be just like Him.

Thank You also for your constant love and wonderful Holy Spirit. He not only burns like a fire at times, but is also the One who comforts so wonderfully and completely. Thank you for the hunger and power He bestows. Without Him, I would not hunger for You nor be able or willing to resist the world, the flesh, and the devil.

Lord, everything I am of any lasting worth is in and of You, and by You alone do I survive and overcome. Please keep on burning away the things in me that don't please You, and strengthening the things that do.

Just as the silversmith melts the ore, skimming away the impurities until he clearly sees his own reflection, so continue to burn and purge, lifting me ever upward into Your purposes, regardless of the cost or pain. Please do this until You see, as it were, Your own reflection when You look at me.

Yes, Lord God, please do make me like Jesus...in every way.

## A Prayer (a poem)

*My heart feels so heavy, my heart feels so low.*
*Lord, I seem to resist and refuse to let go.*
*O God! Change me, Lord, make me swift to hear*
*Your Spirit speaking — Your Spirit so dear.*

*O Jesus my Lord, my Life, my All,*
*may I love You more and answer Your call*
*to take up my cross, to daily die,*
*to cleave always to You, and in You abide.*

*Oh hear me now and change me I pray;*
*may I look unto You each moment of the day.*
*And may You, Lord, transform me till soon all shall see*
*the fullness of Christ ever shining through me.*

*Thank You, O Lord, for Your rest...for Your love...*
*for Your Spirit like fire yet sweeter than a dove...*
*for the hunger He grants and the power He gives.*
*I've my being in You, Lord, and in You I live.*

*So stop not, O Lord, Your refining fire*
*to purge out the dross to bring me yet higher.*
*Yes, never cease, 'ere what it may take,*
*to make me like Jesus, in every way...*

# Our Relationship With Others

*"Do not judge,*
*or you too will be judged.*
*For in the same way you judge others,*
*you will be judged,*
*and with the measure you use,*
*it will be measured to you."*
**Jesus**
**[Matthew 7:1-2; NIV]**

*"If anyone says,*
*'I love God,'*
*yet hates his brother,*
*he is a liar.*
*For anyone who does not love his brother,*
*whom he has seen,*
*cannot love God,*
*Whom he has not seen."*
**[I John 4:20; based on NIV]**

## 28.

# Different Is Not Necessarily Wrong

**There are levels of meaning** and understanding to Scripture. This is not saying that it contradicts itself, because Truth never contradicts Truth, but it is saying that within any number of passages of Scripture there can be various meanings.

However, these various meanings are to be applied at the direction of the Holy Spirit alone! It is not a matter of personal interpretation. The Holy Spirit inspired the Scriptures, and He must interpret them. [See 2 Peter 1:20-21].

As an example of multiple meanings of a certain passage of Scripture (and there are many more), consider Hosea 11:1, where God says that He called His Son out of Egypt. When read in context, the meaning seems obvious — the Lord is apparently referring to delivering His people Israel from the slavery of Egypt. The term "son" is referring to the entire nation, as when many times God referred to at least a remnant of His people as "Jacob." [Numbers 24:5; Isaiah 9:8; 40:27; Jeremiah 30:10; etc.].

**But look!**

In Matthew 2:15 we see a reference to this same passage of Scripture, with the revelation that it was fulfilled when the child Jesus resided with his parents in Egypt for a time, and later returned to Galilee, "called out of Egypt," as it were.

Neither insight is incorrect. Both are perfectly correct. They are both correct because the Holy Spirit chose to apply two different meanings to the same verse.

Please understand me, however. There is no foundational, doctrinal conflict between the two interpretations.
They don't coincide exactly, but neither are they in
conflict: They are simply two distinct, different but
noncontradictory meanings of the same passage of
Scripture.

I wanted to go into some detail with this because I think
it is very important to remember it as we come across
brethren with different insights of certain Scriptures than
what we have. As I touched on previously, this doesn't
mean that the Scriptures can be twisted at our will and
discretion. No, but the Holy Spirit is perfectly capable of
energizing someone else's insight in a different way and
emphasis than He might do with us.

### Still another angle

on "different isn't necessarily wrong" is seen as we
consider what walking in total obedience to our Father
might mean. Our Lord Jesus' life is the only perfect,
untainted example of this, so let's examine it closely. I'm
sure nearly every true follower of our Lord Jesus Christ
would express complete approval of everything that He
did. And wouldn't we all agree that He pleased our
Heavenly Father in everything, at all times?

But it could be one thing to read of events in the Bible,
expressing approval of what is written, and another thing
altogether if we were confronted with some of the same
situations again...

### For example, how would we react

if we actually saw (not just read about) someone
responding to a request for ministry in the realm of
healing of deafness and a speech impediment by first
putting his fingers in the person's ears, then spitting and
touching the needy person's tongue?

Then again, how would we react to seeing someone
making mud from dirt on the ground and their own spit,
then putting the "spitty mud" on a blind person's eyes and
instructing the blind one to go find a certain pool of water

(located in a popular place, during the day, mind you) to wash off the concoction in order to obtain their healing?

Or let's leave out the dirt: What if someone today ministered healing to a blind person by spitting on the person's eyes before laying hands on them???

**Imagine the reaction**

in most gatherings of believers if even one of these things or something similar happened during their next meeting!

What would happen in *our* particular fellowships? Why I believe many in most places would want to do no less than tar and feather the person who indulged in such divergent ministry tactics from the norm. I'm sure many would claim that the one who did such things must certainly be demon possessed.

What would our *own* reaction really be? Let's answer truthfully now!

**As strange as these methods of ministry may seem, they were done by the Lord Jesus. [Mark 7:33; John 9:1-7; Mark 8:23].**

And He Who is "...the same yesterday, today, and forever" (Hebrews 13:8; NKJV) might just do it again (or at least something just as out of the ordinary); this time through His people: the body of Christ.

Now I'm not suggesting that we attempt to move in more shocking ways of ministry. I'm just trying to emphasize that the Lord's ways are often quite different than the ways that men would choose, and we mustn't limit God's expression of His life and will through us, regardless of how strange it may seem to us.

Consider Abraham. Recall his test of being willing to literally kill his son Isaac as a sacrifice to God. No, the Living God was not seeking human sacrifice, but believe me, it sure seemed that way to Abraham when he was being put to the test! [See Genesis 22:1-18].

And as a final example, consider the prophet Hosea. In Hosea 1:2-3, we read that the Lord told Hosea to marry a harlot, which he did. This was a very unique situation in which the Lord wanted to speak to His people through the circumstances of Hosea's life. Nevertheless, the Holy God did command one of His servants to do something that was (and is!) quite out of the usual way He leads His people.

## Now just what would our reaction be

to a brother in the Lord who told us that the Lord wanted him to marry a harlot? What would we really have thought of Hosea if we were living back then and weren't merely reading about his situation from afar, as it were? Then again, what would our response to the Lord be if He told *us* to do the same thing as Hosea, or something similar???

Such considerations may seem scary to us, but they really shouldn't be if we love and trust the Lord purely and completely.

## So where does all of this leave us?

It leaves us helplessly and totally dependent upon the Holy Spirit.

We must "test the spirits" [1 John 4:1-3] and be sensitive at all times to our Father. This will keep us from deception and becoming a close-minded "know-it-all."

If anyone should bring out something from a verse other than what we've seen and we bear witness in our spirit that it is the Truth, we should rejoice. And we shouldn't be quickly discouraged from our original understanding of the verse. Both insights may be correct, with each one to be applied uniquely as the Lord wills.

Also, God's will and leading may seem strange to our natural minds at times, but we can trust Him, knowing that His way is always the best way.

This calls for insight, wisdom, love, and obedient sensitivity.

## REMEMBER:

*Different isn't necessarily wrong!* It might be, but not necessarily!

We are to check it out with the Lord, learning from His Spirit through others as well as directly from Him.

# 29.

# New Wine And Old Wineskins

**You may recall** that in a previous chapter ("The Quest"), it was discussed that many, often with pure motives though clouded vision, are committed to man-made religious systems and organizations. It was also discussed that "he that remains on a sinking ship will with that ship sink!" The segment concluded with a recognition that some may argue that the Lord has them involved in this system of man to reach others in it, perhaps for only a "season," but whether that be so or not, we must always and only follow God's plans, not man's.

Now, I wish to add the following as "food for thought" and as "equipment for action." As with all Truth, if this is for you at this moment, then receive it gladly. If not, leave it before the Lord for Him to do with as He chooses. Just be sure to let all judgment be born of Him...

## John the Baptist

was chosen by God to be used by Him to accomplish a certain task. [Now just as certainly as God had a plan for John's life, He has a particular course already determined that He desires to be followed for every person's life. And if anyone will but follow Him, then that person will automatically follow and fulfill whatever it is that God desires. Each of us should let the "its" of our life develop as the result of our following Him!].

John recognized the call to proclaim the coming of the Messiah, thus bringing an end to the Levitical order, though it had been established by God. [Compare Jeremiah 45:4, where God speaks of breaking down that which He had built, and plucking up that which He had planted. Though the reference is to something else, the principle is the same — the Lord at times has changed His methods of dealing with men without denying His Truth.].

In obedience to God, John went out into the desert rather than follow the established way of doing things.

## What a step that was!

And what a significant lesson for us from which to glean Truth! You see, John, being the son of a priest, was next in his family's line to fill the office of priest. Many, recognizing John's prophetic gift of insight and fiery oratory, probably encouraged John to stay "in the system" and change it from within.

"Look at the influence you'll have, John," they may have said. "There are so many lives you'll be able to touch; so many who will listen to you because of your recognized position. Follow in the footsteps of your father and ancestors. Change things from within the system. Speak this new word from God from within the established order. But John, don't become a renegade, forsaking the way it's always been. Who will listen to you then? Who do you think you are anyway? Don't rock the boat, John."

But John (thank the Lord!) didn't listen to such beguiling and worldly wisdom that may have been offered to him. He recognized that opportunities to minister are not necessarily the leading of God to do so. Therefore, John went forth, forsaking the old to proclaim the new.

## However, let us be quick to add

that although the system and method became obsolete, this does not mean that it did not contain Truth. Truth is Truth, regardless of the validity or lack thereof of its bearer.

## Remember Jesus' point that

"...every teacher of the Sacred Writings who has been instructed about the Kingdom of Heaven is like the owner of a house who brings out of his storeroom new treasures as well as old." [Matthew 13:52; Amplified]. When we read this in light of Matthew 9:16-17, where Jesus warns of putting a new patch on an old garment and also of putting new wine into old wineskins, we see that our Lord validated the Truth of the old system or "container/garment," so to speak, while invalidating the established order and means of containing and presenting the Truth.

God's form of presentation changed, but Truth never changes, for Jesus is the Truth, and He never changes! [John 14:6 and Hebrews 13:8].

Therefore, we see that although God did not want John to put new wine into old wineskins, John's insight did not cause him to constantly rail against the old system and those involved in it. He did attack the mistaken notion that to be involved in "the system" was the same as being involved with God. [Matthew 3:7-9]. But to a much greater degree, his Godgiven insight stirred and emboldened him to get on with the task at hand of preparing people for the new day that was upon them.

*He was more caught up in the glories of the new than the failings and inadequacies of the old!*

If we do the same, this will go a long way in keeping us from haughtiness, arrogance, and a judgmental heart.

We are but servants of God and of those to whom He sends us. We are not to think of ourselves as better than anyone else, regardless of their lack of revelation or maturity.

Let us get on with God and His plans! Any other attitude will only hinder His work, hurting and ultimately destroying our usefulness in His kingdom...

**REMEMBER:**

*New wine doesn't go in old wineskins,*
*but when discarding the old wineskins,*
*don't discard the seasoned wine...*
*Truth is Truth, regardless of the wineskin*
*that contains it!*

# 30.

# Judge Not

**As followers of Jesus Christ,** we are to never condemn or slander anyone, especially our brothers and sisters in Christ. We are to help them in adversity; not bring it on them. [Proverbs 17:17; Galatians 6:2].

Our brethren belong to the Lord, just as we do, and we must love one another dearly, knowing that we do not love the Lord any more than we love His offspring!

Often, we may think another believer is wrong in a given situation, and they might be so; however, when we pass judgment on another based on human reasoning and/or from a critical, mean attitude, we oftentimes become more wrong than they.

For it's not enough just to know the Truth. How we handle the Truth is just as important.

We must be sure to make "righteous judgment," as the Lord Jesus has said. [John 7:24].

## And how do we make righteous judgment?

By hearing from the Spirit of God regarding judgments *He* makes, and letting those judgments alone be ours. Otherwise, we may be rebuked by the Lord as some others were once. [See John 8:15]. We should remember, also, that as we judge, so shall we be judged. [See Matthew 7:1-2].

If He does not reveal something, then we have no right to assume the place of judge. The judgment belongs to God, and we participate in it only if He gives us permission, guided completely by His Spirit. Therefore, we must remain alert to the Spirit of God and in communion with the Lord, not judging "after the flesh." Remember that even Jesus did not speak His own judgments, but only said that which Father told Him to say. [See John 8:26; Amplified].

This insight liberates us and simplifies our lives, for we realize our focus should stay fixed on God's leading in every situation. He alone prepares the hearts of people and grants repentance. One word spoken at His direction and in His Spirit is more powerful than a trillion spoken out of our own choosing and timing!

### Isn't this what the Lord is after anyway?

His desire and intent in all His dealings with us is to cause us to have to deal with and relate to Him personally, drawing every bit of our life from vital, intimate union with Himself. Nothing short of this — opinions, interpretations, and the like — will suffice. From each one of us He seeks and demands relationship — relationship with Himself and His other people, our brethren.

Also, we should move in love, not only towards our brothers and sisters, but also with those in the world. While loving other people does not mean that we always condone their actions and beliefs, it does mean that we "accept" them — faults and all.

We have not been given the right and task of "straightening everybody out" from a wrong, mean attitude.

However, don't misunderstand. If "rhema" — that is, "something spoken by God to someone directly" — comes to us that is a word of judgment against someone or something, then we should speak it with all the might and ability He gives. But if God hasn't spoken, neither should we. In short:

*Let he who speaks speak as an oracle from God! [1 Peter 4:11].*

Another folly and deception we can easily be lured into if we do not walk circumspectly is to put forth a false image of ourselves to other believers. And why are we sometimes prone to do this? Often because our stinking pride desires to make us seem more acceptable or impressive to them.

Instead, we should simply stand in honesty. We need to not only reveal the strengths God has established in us, but also be willing to confess our faults to one another. This will enable us to receive ministry and remain humble, staying in a teachable state of mind and heart. [James 5:16].

## Walk in honesty to walk in light.

Only as we walk in His glorious light will we walk in the fullness of His calling. And only where all things are visible and clear is there light. [Ephesians 5:13b]. To pretend to be something that we are not, even if it is something we or others may truly wish us to be, is to live a lie and walk in darkness and insecurity. God, however, demands honesty from us — we must be guileless and without pretense, walking in "truth," which is "reality." No masks or put-ons (which is hypocrisy) will do.

## We will never change until we admit where we are now.

Though God already knows us, He longs that we pour out everything in our hearts to Him, whether good or bad, righteous or evil. This will pave the way for Him to be glorified in us.

We are able to realize the extent of God's liberating power only as we confess our needs and stand in a place of total and complete honesty and openness before Him. Also, as we stand resolutely, candidly, and honestly in the truth of what and who we are before Him, He will begin to reveal Himself to us.

If we are willing to be known by God, He will be willing to let Himself be known by us. Only as we live unto God and not unto men — seeking His approval instead of a misdirected seeking of men's approval — will we find Him establishing us as honorable before both Himself and our peers.

Let us accept *all* that the Lord has revealed and not pervert the Gospel of our Lord Jesus Christ into "another gospel" of our own making and liking. If we will humble ourselves before God and live unpretentiously and humbly before men, God will work His delight in our hearts and establish us after His own desire.

**The Law of Reciprocity comes into play here:**

If we wish good to come to us, we must give good, for as we sow so shall we reap, whether good or evil. [Luke 6:38; Galatians 6:7-8].

Notice, also, if we are judging another we surely can't be esteeming them as better than ourselves as the Lord commanded us to do. [Philippians 2:3]. Furthermore, the reason anyone would judge another is because they haven't seen the depth of their own depravity!...

Remember Jesus' words: "Why do you look at the speck of sawdust in your brother's eye and pay no attention to the plank in your own eye? How can you say to your brother, 'Let me take the speck out of your eye,' when all the time there is a plank in your own eye? You hypocrite, first take the plank out of your own eye, and then you will see clearly to remove the speck from your brother's eye." [Matthew 7:3-5; NIV].

Therefore, let us leave the judgment up to God, speaking only as He gives us something to speak. After all, He is the only All-Sufficient, Perfect One, and we all — even the most mature of us — need His help at all times so very desperately.

We are in this together, so let's help and not hinder one another.

**Judge Not** (a poem)

*Why do we condemn the ones the Lord has pardoned?*
*Why do we speak against the apple of His eye?*
*While others we accuse, we excuse*
*The greater folly we commit*

*When we judge others when the Lord*
*Has said, "Judge not."*

*Why do we attempt to enhance our reputations*
*by pretending to be something*
*that we've surely never been,*
*instead of being willing to be candid*
*and be honest to confess not only strengths*
*but also faults that are within?*

*Alas! But all too often, due to insecurity,*
*We live a lie per what we think*
*That men would like to see.*
*Let's be done with masks that hide the truth*
*Of what we really are,*
*Thus allowing God the freedom*
*To work changes in our hearts.*

*For as long as we seek praise from men*
*Instead of praise from God,*
*We walk in night, not in the light —*
*In selfishness, not love.*

*For where all things are exposed and open*
*There is glorious light.*
*And where we confess our weakness,*
*God can show us His great might.*

*How foolish not to cling to everything*
*That He's revealed,*
*Like confessing faults and praying*
*So that we all may be healed!*

*So stop judging one another —*
*It will all come back to you;*
*Whether good or evil:*
*It depends on all the things you do.*

*So let's be meek — esteeming others*
*Better than ourselves;*
*And leave the judgment up to God:*
*We all so need His help.*

# 31.

# Listen For The Master's Voice Through ANY Vessel Of HIS Choice *or* It Is Not Our Place To Approve The Vessels God May Choose To Use

**Do you recall** the Biblical account of Balaam and his donkey? [Numbers 22:21-34]. The donkey represents to me a person of the world, symbolizing the fact that God can use even someone not His own to speak to us. We mustn't limit our experiencing God in any given situation due to a limited concept that God only uses His children and not the devil's.

Yes, God can and does use even the devil's children.

Am I promoting the idea that we should seek counsel from the ungodly? Emphatically not! But I *am* saying that we should look to the Lord, and not limit, due to a religious hardening of heart, God's means of accomplishing His purposes.

**Remember the story of Neco,**

the heathen King of Egypt? [2 Chronicles 35:20-24]. He was the acknowledged instrument of God for a certain accomplishment, and when Josiah the godly king attacked him, Josiah was killed, while the heathen was spared!

Also, consider that the Lord Jesus called Judas Iscariot "friend" when Judas came to betray Him [Matthew 26:50], although previously Jesus had referred to Judas as a devil. [John 6:70].

Does this mean that Jesus was showing us to be friends with devils?

**No!**

But He does teach us here that even a devil can be a "friend," so-to-speak, in the sense that he can be used by God to further God's wonderful plan in our lives.

**Years ago,**
this aspect of God's sovereignty was brought home to me as I sat with a man in a hotel lounge...

I belonged to the Lord, and as far as I know, the man was not a believer. Although this was a "worldly" environment, I was not uncomfortable there for two reasons: One, I was in God's will, and, two, God had dealt with me to maintain my rest in Him alone — not the circumstances in which I might find myself.

So, with a mixed-drink in his hand (and lest someone think that I was "downing a few" myself, and therefore encouraging them to do the same — I wasn't), he began to share some of his experiences in business and investments. And as I listened to him, I found myself often exclaiming, "That's such wisdom! Yes, that's wisdom!"

I chose my words carefully because I was recognizing my Heavenly Father's voice and insight coming through this heathen human vessel. And the man did not even know it!

**What a lesson!**

God showed me that He uses whomever and whatever He wills as a tool in His hand and a vessel for His glory. It is not our place to pass judgment upon such matters, but rather to simply look to the Lord, acknowledging His right and ability to do as He pleases.

*How liberatingly simple this wonderful truth is!*

Now we can truly be like the sheep that Jesus said "...hear My voice and will not follow a stranger." [John 10:4-5, 27].

**But what a parodox!**

While we listen for His voice, and not the voice of a stranger, we are aware that He has every right and ability to use a "stranger" (that is, a sinner or what-have-you) through which to speak.

Ha-ha! The goodness and greatness of God's wisdom and the simplicity of the walk He has called us to are wonderful indeed!

# 32.

# The Story Of The Blind Man

**There is a story** of a blind man miraculously receiving his sight and returning to still blind, former associates...

Upon his arrival, he began to tell of the things he now could see, but not in a haughty way, because he knew that his being able to see was a miraculous, unmerited intervention into his situation. However, as he began to describe the way things really are when properly perceived through good eyesight, he was met with ever-increasing intimidations and denouncements from those who were still blind. They were so certain that their opinions were correct that they concluded he was a deluded egomaniac determined to be contentious by not conforming to the "consensus opinion."

This story is not unlike the experience of those who have truly been touched by the Master and determine to pursue Him and stay true to Him and His cause. They will meet with great opposition from those who may claim to see and yet truly do not, whether saint or sinner.

**For this reason,**
let us not be as the blind ones, thinking in the blindness of spiritual pride that we see when we don't. Neither let us succumb to the subtle temptation to think ourselves better than those who have not seen what we have received from the Lord.

Both are great and potentially damnable follies.

"A man can receive nothing except it be given Him from above," [See John 3:27 and Proverbs 2:6]. Therefore, if we do anything or ever see anything in the way of righteousness beyond the finiteness of man's abilities and perceptions, it will always be completely by our God's grace.

Nevertheless, we must not be afraid or ashamed to stand in what we know we've received from God. We just must be sure it is really from God, and not just the parrot-like repeating of truth that we may have heard from others but that hasn't yet been born in our hearts by Him.

Simon was blessed *because* flesh and blood (that is, other people) had not revealed a certain aspect of the Truth to Him, but instead, Jesus' Father in heaven. [Matthew 16:13-17].

### How interesting!

Peter was blessed explicitly because he listened to and received from God instead of men.

"The anointing you have received from Him abides within so that you have no need that any man teach you." [1 John 2:27]. What is this propagating — the elimination of teachers?

In one sense, yes.

That is, we are to look to our Father — our heavenly Daddy, our Papa — not to men. Now Papa, by His Spirit, may choose to speak through someone, but if that person and his listeners are all moving in God's Spirit, then *God's* word (not a word originating from the person God is using) will be both spoken, heard, and received.

### How liberating to know we don't have to "make people see!"

Though we are called to speak God's Word, the "Thus says the Lord!" to our generation, we cannot make others hear. What good is brow-beating someone with some sort of "Christian"(???) brainwashing, so-to-speak, that doesn't affect the heart? We cannot argue His word into them, and any supposed change on their part will not "stick."

I am seeing more and more why Jesus so often said, "He who has ears to hear, let him hear."

So it is still today.

Let us not attempt to abrogate and usurp the office of the Holy Spirit, nor attempt to destroy our listener's free will. As co-laborers with God, we should proclaim only that which He gives us to say with boldness and in love, trusting and allowing Him to work within those who hear us. We know that *God's* Word (as opposed to *our* word) will not return to Him without bearing fruit. [Isaiah 55:10-11].

## How simple and yet profound is this walk in the Spirit of God:

Fearing no man, yet we are to honor all; not conforming simply because it is the norm, and yet, not being a non-conformist just to be different; while looking exclusively to God, we yet acknowledge that we can receive from whomever or whatever He chooses to use.

Yes, the paradoxes of the Kingdom abound and yet produce one kind of life — one hid with Christ in God:

Simple yet profound, straightforward yet sensitive to others, unpredictable yet trustworthy, firm but loving, insightful yet teachable...

May such a life be our longing and constant experience.

# 33.

# Knowing Others — Knowing God

**Often I have cried out to the Lord** to know Him intimately; not vaguely and far away. I used to compare my relationship with the Lord to one that I might have with a loving but distant uncle: someone nice who gave me things, but not someone I'd ever met or known in a deep way. I yearned for the kind of intimacy with the Living God that many people in the Scriptures had. God to them was a living, real Person — Someone with feelings, emotions, and reasoning; Someone Who could communicate and receive communication.

Thank the Lord! He did respond to my prayer and began to let me fellowship with Him more intimately. However, one day while I was working at my job He seemed to say,

"Do you want to get to know Me?"

"Yes, Lord," I replied.

And He said, "Then get to know your brothers and sisters."

**What an eye-opener!**

He began increasing my awareness of a true disciple's relationship with Him: Being joined to God by the Holy Spirit through the blood of Jesus Christ, we are "members of His body, of His flesh and of His bones." [Ephesians 5:30; NKJV]. All who are one with the Lord become one spirit with Him. [1 Corinthians 6:17].

Furthermore, we are astoundingly privileged to be a part of His plan to reveal and impart the knowledge of God to others, since, as His people, we are individually and collectively the temple of God and the body of Christ in and through whom He reveals Himself. [1 Corinthians 3:16; 1 Peter 2:4-5; 2 Thessalonians 1:6-10]. [Also see Chapter 9: "Wonder Of Wonders"].

### How this insight can elevate each of us in one another's eyes in a pure way!

What honor we would bestow upon one another as we really began to grasp what Jesus meant when He discussed that as we treat one of His people, so we are treating Him! [Matthew 25:40; Acts 9:1-4].

Also, we should do our utmost to encourage one another in the Lord and to stir up the impartation of Himself within each other. Not only will this strengthen all of us, but it will also help bring to us a greater revelation of God as we see Him uniquely expressed through the various members of the body of Christ.

And not only should we encourage the revelation of God through others, but each of us should stir up the gift of God within ourself! [2 Timothy 1:6].

To the extent that we deny what and who we are, to the extent that we stifle our own personality and uniquenesses, to the extent we try to "be someone else" that we admire, or deny who we really are in an attempt to fulfill a concept we or others have of spirituality, to that degree we deny ourselves and others Jesus Christ. For He has joined Himself to each of us who have given ourselves to Him, and there is a particular, unique expression and revelation of Himself that can only come through each one of us individually.

This is one reason why we should stop judging one another after the flesh (including ourselves!) and begin to delight in and relish the *differences* in one another. **We need each other!!**

### God's house is made-up of living *stones*, not *bricks*.

Each and every stone is unique; bricks are all alike.

This is one of the wonders of the body of Christ; one of

the ways that "...now, through the Church, the manifold wisdom of God [is being] made known to the angelic rulers and authorities in the heavenly realms..." [Ephesians 3:10; based on NIV and AMP]. Only God can build this temple of such great diversity of experiences and expressions. He will get all the glory!

Each and every member of Christ's body is extremely important — needed to complete this vessel in and through which the Lord Jesus has chosen to reveal and express Himself. That is why the Scripture says that the Church, the body of Christ, is "...the fullness of Him Who fills all in all." [Ephesians 1:23b; AMP].

Yes, as each of us who belong to Jesus know each other better, we will know Him better!

# 34.

# Pastoring Is Parenting *Or*
## True Ministers Are Working Themselves Out Of A Job

**God has always been desirous** of having a people who love Him deeply, know Him intimately, and pursue Him diligently. Furthermore, He longs for this from us individually as well as collectively.

It is true that He has called and anointed certain individuals for specific tasks, equipping them so that they can equip the rest of the Church for ministry. [Ephesians 4:11-16]. But His intention in doing so was not to establish a clergy and laity caste system within the body of Christ.

No! He intends that His ministry flows through *all* of His people; not just a select few.

The ultimate purpose for each member of the body of Christ is the same. We are to love God supremely, with all of our beings, living for His glory, faithfully doing His will in all things, at all times. And we are to be vessels in and through whom the Son of God can express and reveal Himself. Our call is to decrease that the Lord Jesus might increase.

*Every* **member of Christ's body is a minister.**

This is God's design for each and every member of the body of Christ. All of His people are to be able ministers of the New Covenant, regardless of our occupations, vocations, talents, similarities, differences, or ministry emphases.

As we consider all of this, we can understand why *pastoring is a form of parenting*. For you see, a wise and loving parent desires to raise children that grow and develop into mature, responsible individuals who, while maintaining respect and honor for their parents, **do not need**

**them anymore!**

## The Spirit of God made this real to me

in a very practical way. I was playing a game with one of my children. Now at this particular game I am quite an excellent player, and I have discovered some very effective strategies and "secrets." So I was prepared to win the game by a long-shot.

Suddenly, the Spirit of God quickened to me to reveal to my child all my strategies, insights, and secrets. I was to hold nothing back. My "rights" and mastery of the game was to be subjugated to my love for my child, teaching her how to be a master of the game — even if she ended-up surpassing me in her abilities and accomplishments.

My role as a faithful parent is to pour everything I have of any benefit into my children. I am to never gloat over or selfishly cling to any superior knowledge, wisdom, or experience.

## What a lesson it was to me!

Through this simple game, the Lord showed me that — as parents *and* as ministers of the New Covenant — we should do all we can to develop others, holding nothing back that could benefit them. If we are faithful to do this, we will be true servants, and therefore qualified to be leaders amongst God's people. For He who wishes to be first among us must be the servant of all, and whoever desires to be greatest among us must be the slave of all. [See Matthew 20:26-27].

Thus we see why in a very real sense, *true ministers of the New Covenant are working themselves out of a job!*

Look at Ephesians 4:11-13: "It was He [Jesus] Who gave some to be apostles, some to be prophets, some to be evangelists, and some to be pastors and teachers, to prepare God's people for works of service, so that the body of Christ may be built up until we all reach unity in the faith and in the knowledge of the Son of God and become mature, attaining to the whole measure of the fullness of Christ." [Based on NIV].

Notice the words "prepare" and "until." Both of these words stress the points that we have been making: Faithful and true ministers desire to prepare others for ministry. This will continue until the time of maturity of the saints.

At that time, the apostles, prophets, evangelists, pastors and teachers will have truly "worked themselves out of a job!"

## How joyful they will be!

Similarly, how joyful all faithful ministers of the New Covenant are even now when they see other saints mature and not need them as they once did! A wise and faithful minister to God's people delights in witnessing the impartation of the life that they have received take place in the lives of other saints.

Furthermore, we need to stay ever conscious of the fact that *if we cling to our God-ordained ministry in order to maintain our position, the anointing provided for that ministry will destroy us.* The reason for this is because the anointing is for distribution, duplication, and multiplication; not self-fulfillment.

## We should remember:

One person gives to others generously, yet gains even more; then there is another person who holds back from others that which he should give, but it only brings him to neediness and poverty. Also, a generous, giving person will be enriched and prosperous (spiritually as well as materially), and whoever waters and refreshes others will himself be watered and refreshed. [See Proverbs 11:24-25].

Let us all stay determined to pour everything we have received in Christ into others, knowing that *this is the way of the Kingdom of God...*

**In establishing others we are established, and in giving we receive!**

# 35

# The Strength Of The Whole Is Dependent On The Strength Of The Parts

**Many speak of "the corporate anointing."** This is "that anointing which God grants to His people as they gather together in unity and singleness of mind and heart unto Him." It is true that this anointing does strengthen the individual members of the body of Christ. However, the manifestation, experience, and purity of any corporate anointing is directly related to the maturity, strength, and yieldedness to God's Spirit on the part of the *individuals* that make up the corporate group.

Only with complete consecration, focus on, and obedience to the Lord on the part of the individual members of the body of Christ will there ever be the kind of corporate anointing that He has promised and so longs to bring to fruition. This anointing will enable Him to be revealed through His people in fullness, and not just in measure.

Each one of us who are His people, as an individual member — one of the "members in particular" — of the body of Christ, is being urged by the Spirit of God to grow up and fulfill our calling. This calling consists of coming to intimately know the Lord and display our own unique expression of the union of God's Spirit with our spirit.

Though God has appointed those whose duty it is to oversee the flock of God, He is a judge of men's hearts and is not impressed by the positions that men hold. [Galatians 2:1-6]. There is only one mediator between God and man — the Man Christ Jesus [1 Timothy 2:5], and He has made *all of those* that belong to Him a kingdom of priests to serve God. [See Revelation 1:6; NAS]. Though we all have different functions in the body of Christ, each one of us is special and precious to the Lord.

**Years ago,**

while traveling with "The Sharrett Brothers," a music ministry team, we sang and spoke on a Saturday night and the following Sunday morning at a Baptist fellowship. During our Saturday night meeting, it was announced that a couple of us had gone to a certain Bible college.

Later that evening, while in bed, the Lord gave me a prophecy which I felt impressed to write down. The next day, I saw His wisdom and plan in doing this...

You see, on Sunday we had a time of sharing, and I read this prophecy to them, encouraging them to listen to it as though the Lord was speaking to them (which, of course, He was). Being Baptist, the majority of them, if not all, would have been perhaps offended or even confused if I had just launched into a spontaneous, extemporaneous prophecy. However, by my reading it to them, they were able and willing to receive it.

Anyway, after our meeting, someone came up who really enjoyed what I said, and he commented to me that I must have been one of those who had gone to that Bible college that had been mentioned the previous night.

Thank the Lord, I was able to point this person exclusively to the Lord, and give all the glory to Him...

"No," I said. "The Lord is speaking to whoever has ears to hear. He'll speak to you if you'll listen."

I wanted him to see God's speaking to someone is not based on a certain type or level of education in the schools of men, or whether you have a recognized title in the religious world.

No, His speaking to someone is predicated on His grace and the person to whom He is speaking being willing to hear.

**The sheep are to lead the lambs to the Shepherd:**

Jesus' sheep hear His voice and will not follow a stranger. [John 10:3-5].

### But notice:

*Sheep follow the Shepherd and lambs follow sheep!*

All of God's people are called to relate to the Great Shepherd of the sheep, the Lord Jesus. However, the more mature ones of the fold — that is, "the sheep" — have come to the point where they recognize the Shepherd's voice.

But the lambs have not yet learned to distinguish the Shepherd's voice from others'. Therefore, they often rely on the leadership of the sheep, but are to do so for only as short a time as is necessary!

No, we don't become renegades, totally independent of each other. We are to always be *inter*dependent, exhorting and helping one another individually and corporately. But by their instruction and example, the sheep are to teach and train the lambs who follow them how to hear and follow Jesus the Shepherd.

### The sheep are not to take His place!

They are to be like the Apostle Paul who encouraged some to be followers of him, just as he was a follower of Christ [1 Corinthians 11:1], and yet he longed to present each individual complete and mature in Christ. [Colossians 1:28].

### Each of us are to know the Lord intimately

[See Jeremiah 31:31-34] and able to help others do the same. There will yet be "one flock under one Shepherd" manifested! [John 10:16; Amplified].

All of us are to be looking exclusively to Him, and intently and expectantly at Him.

Our lives should be moving in worship, God's power, and His love. We ought to be speaking His words constantly, moment-to-moment walking in His paths, and following His directions.

Others within and without the body of Christ need the

Lord's ministry through *each* of us, regardless of our individual uniquenesses.

Let us be faithful to the Lord every moment of every day, becoming strong and mature in His Spirit. Then, more than seeking blessings, we will be people who seek to bless!

# 36

# The Anointing And Spiritual Authority

**I recall a time a number of years ago** when the Lord brought home to me some insight regarding spiritual authority and its proper function:

During praise and worship with a fellowship of believers, the Lord gave me a prophecy to deliver to the people. As I began to give it, a lady in attendance began to speak quite loudly in tongues.

So, I just raised my volume a bit more.

However, so did she.

I glanced at her briefly during my delivery, and she seemed oblivious to the order of the meeting (or the lack thereof that she was causing!). I tried once more to speak out louder than her, hoping that she would hush and wait for a more opportune time, but to no avail. She, on the contrary, only got louder.

Finally I just looked at her, and *I* shut up!

Afterwards, one of the "team members" accompanying me (we were invited to minister to this congregation) said, "Larry, I sure felt for you, man. That lady was so far out of line. I wanted to say something, but since we were just visitors, and the pastor or no one else said anything, I didn't feel like I should do anything."

**Instantly these words came from my lips,**

and I believe they came from the Spirit of God: "If a man is a prophet, then he is a prophet to the whole body!"

While this statement addresses the prophetic office specifically, I'm certain that God was conveying a general principal of the Kingdom that applies to every member of Christ's body:

If you are called of God, that calling is a part of you wherever you go. You don't put it on and take it off like a garment. It is only the leading and anointing of the Spirit of God that should determine when and how you are to function in His gifts or your calling, not some "turf consciousness."

**We are to follow God and not fear men's displeasure towards us for obeying Him.**
[See Jeremiah 1:8, 17; Ezekiel 2:6; Luke 12:4-5; 2 Timothy 1:6-7; Hebrews 13:6].

I exhorted my friend that if he was convinced that God wanted him to deal with the situation by correcting the lady that was out of order, it certainly would not have been wrong for him to obey God, following His leading. He would not have been overstepping his boundaries, because:

*The anointing and leading of God carry His authority!*

We need to enlarge our vision to see that we are a part of the universal body of Christ; joined to and in need of every member of Christ's body everywhere (and they need us, too!). Whenever we gather with *any* of the saints *anywhere,* we are with family and are "at home," and should be willing to not only *receive* ministry from others, but also willing, open, and desirous to *give* ministry to others.

**Also, the Lord Jesus is wanting us to grasp His goal**
of there being "...one flock under one Shepherd." [John 10:16b; AMP]. This of course doesn't mean that we all have to meet together at one time, nor does this insight do away with the "local assembly" and commitment to those to whom God brings us into relationship on a personal level. It also does not imply that God has done away with His plan to use apostles, prophets, evangelists, pastors, teachers, and others to develop and equip us and the other members of the body of Christ for ministry. [Ephesians 4:8-16; 1 Corinthians 12:4-28].

Nevertheless, we need to keep pressing for the goal and vision that God has determined for us, and not on the tools and means that He utilizes to get us there! If we keep our eyes and hearts on God's ultimate, unchanging plan for the present — the goal of a pure, undefiled and united people in and through whom the Son of God can express and reveal Himself — the tools (the intermediary people and things) will all find their proper roles and places in our lives.

**Remember:** *The anointing and leading of God carry His authority!*

# Our Walk In This Hour: A Time Of Maximum Earnest!!!

*"But the Day of the Lord will come
like a thief, and then
the heavens will vanish with a roar
and the elements will be destroyed
with intense heat,
and the earth and everything in it
will be laid bare and burned up.*

*"Since all these things are
to be destroyed in this way,
what sort of people ought you to be?
You ought to live holy and godly lives,
looking forward to the Day of God
and hastening its coming.*

*"That Day will bring about
the destruction of the heavens by fire,
and the elements will melt
with intense heat!*

*"But He has promised
new heavens and a new earth,
the home of righteousness,
and we are looking forward to this.*

*"Therefore, beloved,
since you are looking forward
to all these things,
make every effort to be found
spotless, blameless, and at peace with the Lord."*
***[2 Peter 3:10-14; based on NIV and NAS]***

# 37.

# The Day of the Lord

**The "Day of the Lord" is upon us** — that time when God shall utterly shake and shatter the illusions that mankind has lived for in its adamant refusal to seek Him, love Him, and walk in His ways. Every haughty look and proud, self-sufficient heart in all its pomp and pride will be laid low!

Regardless of how grandiose and lofty man's accomplishments and intents have been, God shall show how futile and temporal they are when they do not stem from intimate relationship with Himself. Therefore, God, Who is "a consuming fire" [Hebrews 12:29], shall engulf and destroy the false precepts and deceptive accomplishments of men. This He will do as He more dramatically begins to intervene in the affairs of mankind during this closing hour of the present age.

**Soon it will be history:**

God's fearful and thorough judgments shall completely overtake and overwhelm those who live in rebellion against Him.

Whether this state of rebellion is blatant, stiffnecked, and conscious, or evidenced by lax indifference, it produces similar results — a life that is not in conformity with God's purposes and plans. Such a life is painful and always leads to destruction.

Specifically, this rebellion is a refusal to choose to heed God's call to accept, obey, love, and seek to know His Son, the Lord Jesus Christ.

### The Day Of Judgment is upon us.

Yes, soon, in spite of man's foolish and damning choice to turn from God, the Lord Jesus will return as He said, and everyone will stand openly exposed before God and His creation. Even the things men thought were either well hidden in their hearts or done in secret will be shown and declared before everyone! [Luke 8:17; 12:2-3; Romans 2:16; 1 Timothy 5:24-25]. God shall do this by the power that enables Him to sit enthroned, unthreatened over all His creation.

Let us not, therefore, live our lives for the purpose of heaping to ourselves the fleeting, temporal tokens that this present world can offer. Instead, let our life's goal and motivation be to perceive and pursue the things eternal and unseen.

In other words, let us live in this physical domain without being satiated with it. Rather, we should live as strangers in a foreign land, knowing that our citizenship is in Heaven.

### The "Test":

One day our Heavenly citizenship will be openly revealed, but now, for the most part, it is kept hidden from our human consciousness as a critical part of "the test."

Living *in* this present world, but living *for* the one soon to come: This is the test.

We should seek "the things unseen." These are "...the things above, where Christ is, seated at the right hand of God." [Colossians 3:1; NAS]. This is the eternal realm of God's manifested presence and kingdom.

### "True" Faith:

Only by maintaining the perception and pursuit of "the things unseen" will we ever please God. For without "faith," which is "the perception and pursuit of the Kingdom of God," it is impossible to please Him. "For whoever would come near to God must believe that God exists (though invisible), and that He is the Rewarder of those who diligently seek Him." [See Hebrews 11:6, 27; and 10:32-34; based on AMP].

God brings to bear great dealings in people's lives. His intent is that they would turn to Him and grow in their understanding of, love for, and ability to reveal His temporarily unseen kingdom and His uncompromising standards of right and life.

### Don't be slack.

We must not, therefore, become overtaken with any amount of spiritual lethargy and sluggardness, producing conformity to the standards and codes of this temporal world order.

No, we must be diligent to cry out to the Lord, express our desire for Him (or at least the desire to have the desire!) and live in the awareness that soon God will reward those who have loved Him and "passed the test," so-to-speak, by living *in* this visible, temporal, physical realm, while loving and living *for* the realities of the invisible, eternal, spiritual realm.

### Great Power — *God's Power* — To Be Released:

Psalm 110:3 says, "Your people shall be willing in the day of your power...." *This,* the Day of the Lord, *is* the day of God's power!

And at this time, those who seek the Lord in Truth and sincerity shall offer themselves willingly to the Lord to do His bidding. They shall come forth as a mighty army, empowered by the Spirit of God to fully accomplish His victorious will and triumph over all His enemies.

Yes, God will soon cause to flood forth a mighty torrent and expression of His life through willing and obedient vessels. This anointing of His Spirit shall strengthen both them and others throughout their entire beings.

Those chosen for such an expression of God's life shall be those who have made their "calling and election sure" [2 Peter 1:10] by refusing to accept the standards of this fading and doomed world system. Instead, they will have turned and given themselves to God completely, listening to and obeying every word that He speaks to them.

These are those who even now are making themselves ready by their utter dependency on God, and who accept joyfully the will of God, regardless of the pain or cost involved. Thus they manifest the Kingdom of God in their particular life's circumstances.

## And what is the Kingdom of God?

*It is the will of the Father fully and perfectly expressed.*

These overcoming ones shall heed the grace of God which teaches us to say **"No"** to all ungodliness [Titus 2:11-14] — all desires and ambitions that destroy one's perception of, love for, and pursuit of the Kingdom of God.

These distractions will always come as: 1) the lust of the flesh — physical desires that scream for precedence over wisdom and godliness, 2) the lust of the eyes — setting our hearts on things seen instead of on the things unseen above, where Christ is; and creating mental fantasies that deprive one of experiencing reality, and 3) the pride of life — that state-of-mind-and-heart that causes us to trust in our own abilities and the riches and false securities of the world. This will always lead to proud, boastful, self-assertive and self-confident attitudes that take us away and cut us off from God's presence.

## But knowing these things is not enough!

Mentally assenting as to the validity of any aspect of the Truth does not necessarily mean that we have embraced it, put it into practice, and thereby made it a vibrant part of our life.

## *We must choose to obey God — He will meet us there.*

It is *our choice* coupled with *His power* that will enable us to live for what these physical eyes and minds cannot perceive nor conceive.

We must not set our hearts on this dead and doomed world that screams for our attention and fights for our affections.

Most generations have chosen to love the things that are seen rather than the things that are unseen. Still, all of God's presently suffering creation eagerly awaits our choice, for therein lies the determining factor whether God will use *us* in accomplishing His intent for this hour.

You and I must make — continually — a choice, either to follow God's wonderful, though oftentimes difficult, hard-to-understand way, or our own petty, selfish, painful and inevitably deadly way.

**What is *our* choice?**

God Himself waits, though not much longer, for our response...

**THE DAY (Of The Lord),
THE CALL (Of Pursuit),
THE CHOICE (Of Preparedness).** (a poem)

*The Day is coming (It is now at hand)
When all will fail that was made by man.
His hopes, his dreams, his deep desires
Will be consumed within God's fires.*

*[With vengeance keen, without relent
The Lord His awesome judgments sent
To burst upon the careless ones
Who do not seek the Lord God's Son.]*

*And soon, though most refuse to hear
The Lord shall come and men shall fear
Before the righteous, searching eye
Of the Mighty God Who reigns on high.*

*Seek not, therefore, the earthly things
Which only briefly pleasure bring
But seek the lasting, unseen goal —
Let **this** pursuit consume your soul.*

*For God the hearts of men does test*

*And longs that they would seek His best*
*Turning from their selfishness*
*To seek God's Kingdom and Righteousness.*

*Let not, therefore, your heart grow cold*
*Nor be conformed by this world's mold.*
*Instead, pursue the Lord with love*
*And set your heart on things above.*

*For purer life than what we've seen*
*Shall soon come forth through vessels clean*
*Who earnestly God's word apply;*
*Who take their cross and daily die...*

*The call has come, the way is clear*
*Will we obey or refuse to hear?*
*Will we pass the test and be able to stand*
*In the presence of the Son of Man?*
*Or will we, as most in the past*
*Cling to the things that will not last?*

*Our choice creation groans to see —*
***Will God be pleased with you and me?***

# 38.

# Walk The Talk

**There is a familiar saying,** "Your actions speak so loud, I can't hear a word you're saying!"

Many people are good at "*talking* a fine line," but not "*walking* a fine line."

In this hour, God is shaking everything that can be shaken. [Hebrews 12:26-27]. If our life is one of hypocrisy, then it is built on a weak foundation, and we will be shaken and will fall!

Remember, Jesus said, "Whoever hears these words of mine and *does* them — putting them into practice — is like a wise man who built his house on a rock." [See Matthew 7:24]. That "house," that life, will stand, unshaken and solid.

Only by walking (not just talking) with the Lord will we ever please Him and walk in the fullness of His love and power. Our obedience in word *and* action is of critical importance. Christ's death and resurrection for us was done to work a total and complete change, even "re-creation," in us. [2 Corinthians 5:17]. His desire is that we *walk out our profession and work out our salvation.* [Philippians 2:12].

**Of The Heart — Not Just The Head:**

Our doctrine and relationship with God must be more than head knowledge, wishful thinking, or positive confession. It must be true reality in our hearts which permeates our entire beings and lifestyles.

God is not looking for mere talkers, but walkers.

He is not looking merely for preachers and teachers with only a good word. Instead, He is searching for "reachers" who will reach out and effect changes in other lives by both their words *and* deeds.

**Reality — Not Hypocrisy:**

They who are dead in their sins [Ephesians 2:1-3] will be hindered from receiving the word of life regarding the Gospel of the Kingdom of Jesus Christ if the person delivering that word is living a lie — saying one thing, but not living it; not putting it into their practical experience.

Yes, if we don't live what we talk about, that is, if we don't "practice what we preach," our words will tend to fall on deaf ears, because people will usually turn away from a hypocrite. And if we talk one way, while living another way, that's exactly what we are — hypocrites.

**People need more than rhetoric.**

They need positive action and a demonstration of the Holy Spirit and power. [1 Corinthians 2:4].

When someone who shares God's Word does not embrace the Truth that they speak, if they don't "walk the talk," their words are made empty. Their witness becomes tainted. Their pure word becomes mixed with that which is defiled, hence, it becomes diluted and polluted.

Remember that a lot of clear water added to dirty water still produces dirty water; but only a small amount of dirty water added to clear water renders the mixture dirty. "Dead flies make a perfumer's oil stink, so a little foolishness is weightier than wisdom and honor." [Ecclesiastes 10:1; NAS].

It is true that "the gifts and callings of God are without repentance" [Romans 11:29] — He does not take them back — and even through tainted vessels, God often speaks and pours forth His power. It is also true that God's word will not return to Him "void;" that is, "of no effect," or "fruitless." [Isaiah 55:11]. God's word will accomplish that for which it was sent, even though the vessel delivering that word may be unclean.

Nevertheless, an impure, hypocritical child of God is cheating himself and others from a most blessed gift and experience — the fullness of the anointing that comes forth from those who maintain a constant intimacy with the Lord through their faith and obedience.

**The hour is late. The day is at hand.**

The Day of the Lord has come upon us, and it is a time of consideration and preparation. It is a time to make our calling and election sure and steadfast, without any compromise whatsoever.

Let us pour out our hearts to God and love Him with all of our beings. If we are playing games with the things of God, it must stop. This is serious business, with eternal ramifications. We are to love our brethren and stir up the gifts resident by His Spirit within us. We are to be the salt of the earth and the light of the world.

**Only the pure in heart shall see God. [Matthew 5:8].**

Only those who live and give forth the Truth without compromise or hypocrisy shall experience the depths of the knowledge *of* the Lord, not just *about* the Lord. "The secret of the Lord belongs to those who fear Him..." [Psalm 25:14a]. Those who fear the Lord God walk in His ways and hate evil [Proverbs 8:13], pursuing Him diligently.

Let us take heed to walk in that which we proclaim to others regarding the way of Righteousness and Truth. They that not merely talk the walk, but who also walk the talk shall greatly increase their effectiveness in finding rest for their own souls, ministering to others, and delighting the heart of the Lord Jesus!

**Remember:** We must not just talk the walk; we must WALK the TALK!


**Walk The Talk** (a song)

*Give a listen to me people.*
*Hear what I am telling you.*
*Many speak but don't say nothin',*
*'cause they don't really follow through.*
*But you know there is a shaking —*

*Shaking everything untrue.*
*And we'll see what is important*
*Is not just what we say, but what we do.*

(Chorus) *We gotta walk the talk*
*We gotta walk the walk*
*Not just talk the walk*
*We got to walk the talk!*

*So be sure your revelation*
*Is in your heart — not just your head.*
*And always live the Truth you're speakin'*
*Or you'll not give life to the dead.*
*For they won't hear what you're sayin'*
*If you don't practice what you preach.*
*Your words must be backed-up with action*
*If others you want to reach.*

(Chorus) *We gotta walk the talk*
*We gotta walk the walk*
*Not just talk the walk*
*We got to walk the talk!*

(Bridge) *Behold the people!*
*They have lost their way.*
*They're needing examples.*
*And not just words we say!!*

(Chorus) *We gotta walk the talk*
*We gotta walk the walk*
*Not just talk the walk*
*We got to walk the talk!*

# 39.

# Warriors Of God *or*
## You Can't Experience A Victory Unless You Go Through A Battle

**The Lord** is certainly not limited to speaking to us only during designated prayer times or only at certain locations. One of the first times He spoke to me, I was in the shower!

I can remember it so distinctly because *it* was so distinct and unexpected. Like a ticker-tape going across my mind came words with great clarity and emphasis. I began hollering to my roommate to come into the bathroom so I could tell him through the shower curtain what the Lord had just told me. This is what the Lord said:

"You can't experience a victory unless you go through a battle!"

**Wow!**

It had a tremendous impact on me, yet I didn't begin to fully comprehend those words until a short while later, when the greatest and most intimate revelation of God I had ever known was granted to me, *after* He had brought me through the most difficult time of my life that I had yet experienced.

People like to feel good, and therefore, they are sometimes prone to neglect the seriousness and urgency of our call. Instead, they often go for a more enjoyable, "easy" way of life and doctrine that focuses on God's blessings for *us* rather than on how we can be a blessing to and for *Him*.

We must realize that although this walk with God is

laced with many blessings from Him, His plan and purpose for us is that we would satisfy *His* will, not ours. He wants us to become completely committed to Him and His kingdom. Then He can train us to become stalwart warriors of God, engaging in and winning every battle that we shall frequently have with the powers of darkness.

**Serious Business:**

What we are involved in is serious business — life and death — whether we recognize it or not. Our enemy is determined and crafty, and our God desires to train and use us to completely rout the enemy and devastate his kingdom and plans. As long as we are self-seeking and not focused completely on the Lord, we can never be molded by His Spirit into a unified and invincible fighting force that shall strike terror in the hearts of the powers of darkness and bring defeat to them.

**The Pains That Bring Gains:**

It is through "growing pains" that our natural life develops into maturity, and, like the Son of God did, we learn obedience, developing spiritual maturity, through the things that we suffer. [Hebrews 5:8]. Our spiritual being — our eternal essence — is developed oftentimes through the pain of confrontations with Satan and his demons, other people, the circumstances of life, our own selves, and even God Himself. "It is through much tribulation that we enter the Kingdom of God." [Acts 14:22].

Remember, for the joy He knew would be His afterwards, our Lord Jesus endured the cross while despising the shame. [Hebrews 12:2]. That is, because of His unshakeable belief and confidence in His Father, His kingdom, and His promises, Jesus our Lord was willing to obediently suffer death upon a cross while scorning or ignoring the shame of such a death. He gave the shame no place in His being.

It's not that He was seething with hatred towards the shame. It's just that the shame did not compare to the joys and fulfillment that were His *as* He accomplished God's will and *for* accomplishing God's will.

Likewise, each one of us, knowing by faith that a crown of righteousness awaits the victors, and reward beyond our comprehension awaits the overcomers, must endure every moment in this life like a good soldier with the strength and vigor of the Holy Spirit. [See 2 Timothy 2:3; 4:7–8; 1 Corinthians 2:9–10; Revelation 2:7, 11, 17, 26-29; 3:4-6, 12-13, 21-22].

In the spiritual as well as the physical realm, the taste and thrill of victory is so much sweeter, exciting, and fulfilling the more fierce, intense, and challenging the conflict is.

But don't misunderstand me. Of a certainty, Jesus Christ has already secured, through His sacrificial death and resurrection, the victory over every enemy of Truth and Righteousness.

However, much of the enforcing of this victory is to be done by the Church so that God's people can grow in their knowledge of God and be further developed in their preparation for ruling with Christ.

## The Angels Are Stepping Aside.

Even now, in the unseen, spiritual realm, angelic hosts who were at the forefront of the conflict against the fallen angels are stepping aside, allowing the Church to take the lead and front-line position in the warfare. They will help us, but we are to head-up the battle with the Lord Jesus as our Captain and Commander-In-Chief. We are to stand strong in the Lord and in the power of His might. [Ephesians 6:10; NKJV]. The overcomer, "the victorious fighter," shall be granted the priceless honor of sitting with Jesus Christ "on His throne," (a symbol of authority and rulership), just as Jesus Christ, the Lamb and Lion, overcame and was granted the right to sit with His Father on His throne. [Revelation 3:21].

Remember, our Leader and Example, the Lord Jesus, set His face determinedly, unmovably, "like a flint," [Isaiah 50:4-7] towards His Father and His Father's will.

Facing His Father and His Father's will are one in the same:

You can't accept one without the other.

So though we may suffer a little while, our reward is great and indescribable. And our suffering is eased through the Holy Spirit Who comes to live within every true child of God. It is likewise eased through the comfort of the Son of God Who entered into conflict with this temporal world order, defeating it and bringing to nothing its power. [John 16:33]. All those who come to Him are empowered to walk in the completeness of His victory over all the works and deceits of the world, the flesh, and the devil. They will be able to do this as long as they cling constantly to the Lord Jesus, obeying Him instantly.

## So be encouraged, O warriors of God!

Though we are weak and ineffectual apart from Jesus, in and through Him we are strong and victorious. How glorious to know that though battles are still being fought, the war is won!

*It is finished!*

The next time we engage in conflict, let us rejoice, because the conflict is the pathway to greater heights in God. As we stand in His victory and overcome His enemies, we will be brought into a greater awareness of God's kingdom.

REMEMBER: **"You can't experience a victory unless you go through a battle!"**

# 40

# Focus On JESUS In Faith — NOT On Circumstances In Fear

**It seems as though** many think that great faith is shown by making a great deal of noise, bombarding heaven with requests for help and intervention into their circumstances. "Surely the Lord will be pleased if we cry out to Him, acknowledging how desperate and needy we are for Him to help us in this situation," some of us reason.

But such is not always the case...

The twelve apostles were becoming more and more terrified of the terrible storm at sea, so much so that they even began fearing for their lives. In frantic terror they awakened Jesus. He had been sleeping at the front of the boat.

"Lord, save us!" they pleaded.

"We're going to die!"

Jesus did save them, and, no, it wasn't their time to die. Afterwards, however, instead of praising them for calling on His name, He rebuked them!...

Matthew 8:24-26 and Mark 4:37-40 are passages of Scripture that describe this storm at sea episode. The apostles probably thought that it was an act of faith in Jesus to awaken Him and beg Him to save them. But quite to the contrary, as we've seen, Jesus was not impressed with their calling on Him. He promptly rebuked them for their lack of faith. And Mark's account even records that He rebuked them for having *no* faith.

**"But how can this be?" we might ask.**

"They confessed their need of Him!" Yes, but they were frantic, fearing for their lives.

True faith in Jesus in this instance would have rested

quietly in the knowledge that He was with them, they were in His will, and therefore, they had no need to fear. The fear and tormenting turmoil that they expressed showed that their prayer was from a wrong perspective and attitude of heart — not one of faith. Though they called on the Lord, they were not really trusting Him...

A confession of need and a prayer for help are not proofs of faith. To the contrary, at times they reveal the lack or absence of faith!

**These words, found in Isaiah, are very appropriate here:**

"For thus said the Lord God, the Holy One of Israel, 'In returning to Me and resting in Me you shall be saved; in quietness and in (trusting) confidence shall be your strength.' " [Isaiah 30:15; Amplified].

*Faith in God breeds confidence in God.* He is the One absolutely sufficient for all our needs.

True faith is always focused on God and His Son, not on the circumstances of life.

Getting "off-focus," not centered on Jesus, was the reason that Peter began to sink after walking on the water at Jesus' command. [Matthew 14:23-33]. Peter got his eyes off of Jesus, onto the wind and waves, and, becoming afraid, he began to sink. Jesus saved him, and then, just as He did to all twelve apostles after the storm at sea, He rebuked Peter for having only a little faith and for doubting Him. He was disturbed that Peter did not maintain his confidence in Him.

Granted, in both the storm at sea and in Peter's situation, they who were in need did cry out to Jesus to save them. They did recognize His ability to do so, as well as their absolute inability to save themselves. Also, no other "deity" (so called) was called upon — Jesus was recognized as the only source for deliverance and safety. For all this they can be commended.

But let us not miss the point. Jesus was (and is) in the process of developing His people in their inner man, and, therefore, what many might think is an expression of faith is often taken quite the opposite by the Lord, and therefore rejected by Him.

### The lesson here is this:

*Before* the deliverance from trying and difficult circumstances, the Lord Jesus wants us confident of absolute victory and full of joy while still in them! This we can do only if our hearts with their affections and our minds with their thoughts are kept centered and focused on Him!

"You [Lord] will keep him in perfect peace, whose mind is stayed on You, because he trusts in You. Trust in the Lord forever, for in YAH, the Lord, is everlasting strength." [Isaiah 26:3-4; New King James Version].

### Remember:

Faith is the perception and pursuit of "the things unseen," which is all that pertains to the Kingdom of God. Therefore, if we maintain this perception and pursuit, we will abide in overcoming joy and peace, even in the midst of dreadful ordeals!

### *O God, help us in this we pray, in Jesus' name!*

So we see that "faith in Jesus," in this sense, means "having confidence in Him beyond anything else, keeping our heart's attention and pursuit set upon Him." We sin when we do not stay fixed and focused on Jesus, putting less confidence in Him than we do in other things.

Therefore, we must never forget to keep our focus on Him. Also, we must be on our guard to not be deceived into thinking we are moving in faith when in reality we are moving in fear — the opposite direction...

*Whenever fear of circumstances is in control, then faith is not present!*

### Focus (a poem)

*Please lift my eyes to higher realms*
*where grace and truth abound*
*Where lesser things all fade away*

*and You alone are found.*

*Please cause my ear to only hear*
*the words You speak to me*
*That I might walk in holiness*
*and constant victory.*

*Erase, Lord, from my heart*
*the paths and fantasies of night*
*My mind renew with thoughts of You*
*and flood me with Your light.*

*For I know that you bid me, "Come,"*
*through threatening storms of hell*
*But if I keep my eyes on You*
*I always shall prevail.*

*For perfect peace You've promised those*
*whose thoughts are stayed on You*
*And if I hear and heed Your Word*
*I'll not go down but through.*

*I will to do Your will and keep my focus set and keen*
*On You — my Life.*
*Oh! By and in and through me, Lord, be seen!*

# Epilogue

*"We must pay more careful attention, therefore,
to what we have heard,
so that we do not drift away."*
**[Hebrews 2:1; NIV]**

*"...guard what has been entrusted to you."*
**[From 1 Timothy 6:20; NIV]**

*"Guard the good deposit that was entrusted to you —
guard it with the help of the Holy Spirit Who lives in us."*
**[Based on 2 Timothy 1:14; NIV]**

*"Dear friends, I urge you,
as aliens and strangers in the world,
to abstain from sinful desires,
which war against your soul."*
**[1 Peter 2:11; NIV]**

# 41.

# Closing Thoughts

**Some, after reading this book, may say,** "Great, so I hear what you're saying. I see what you mean. But sum it up for me with some clear, concise direction:

"*How* do I fulfill the highest calling of all?

"*How* do I get to know the Lord intimately?

"*How* do I walk in the fullness of His holiness, love, and power?"

I must be careful here to not attempt to reduce life to a formula, for it cannot be done. Life would cease to be life. It would cease being liquid. Flowing. Spontaneous.

It would become dead. Stagnant. Predictable.

Life, real life, God's life, is not that way.

**As He has shared with me, I now share with you:**

Walk in the light that you have, and ask the Lord for more.

Live each moment in the awareness of His existence.

Be done with lying religious notions, thinking that you must be in a certain place at a certain time with certain people dressed a certain way to fellowship with the Living God.

**No!**

He sees each situation in your life. He hears your every word.

He knows your every thought, motive, desire, need, wish, and longing.

His Presence is wherever you are, for He fills all things. [Ephesians 1:23]...

...So, right now and always, open up to Him, receiving His life and love in the name of Jesus Christ His Son.

Pour out your heart to Him, and don't allow yourself to be deceived into thinking that you can hide anything from Him.
You can't.

Do not lie. Be honest with God, yourself, and others.

Walk the talk and talk the walk.

Settle for nothing less than the Living God and His Son, Jesus Christ, being made real to you and becoming intimate with you.

Stir yourself to focus on and worship Jesus Christ. The Father and the Spirit delight to see the Son glorified.
So call upon Him now and always.

Live a life worthy of the Lord: Pure. Holy. Not being ashamed to stand in the Truth.

Love His Word. Meditate on it, obey it, and speak it.

Fellowship with and love His people. As you get to know them, you will get to know Him.

Help others in need, and don't become bitter if they can't or won't pay you back. Instead, trust in the Lord, looking to Him and casting all of your cares upon Him.

Do not judge others. God alone is the Judge.

Don't try to be something you're not. When you deny and stifle your uniquenesses and personality, you deny Him, for He has joined Himself to you, and that union is unique. There is no one else just like you in and through whom He can reveal Himself.

Never allow yourself to be proud, haughty, or boastful...

. . . Remember, God can still speak through jackasses.
So where does that leave us?
In need of Him.
He alone deserves *all* the praise and glory.

Pray at all times. That is, keep your "line" open to God always. Talk to Him at any time, about anything.

Be aware that many times you must resist the devil, not just try to "think about something else" or change your circumstances.

The devil is as real as God.

But God, of course, has defeated him through the cross.

We now overcome him by the blood of the Lamb and the word of our testimony. [Revelation 12:11].

Speak to Satan, therefore, boldly and out-loud, if possible. Resist him in the name of Jesus and speak-forth an appropriate Scripture that "fits" the situation. For God's word is the Sword of the Spirit. Spoken from the lips of a heart submitted to God, it strikes fear in the heart of the enemy, bringing into your situation his defeat at the cross.

Just remember: Speaking the name of Jesus or certain Scriptures is no "magic wand." Recall that seven sons of a man named "Sceva" tried to use the name of Jesus to cast some demons out of a man once. These seven did not have a relationship with Jesus as their Sovereign Lord, and the demons nearly killed them! [Acts 19:14-16]. So don't bear the name of Jesus lightly.

Don't fret or worry. To do so is harmful and sinful.

Don't hold grudges. If a brother or sister offends you, go to them and try to work it out.

Don't make life complicated. Face a day at a time, and trust in the Lord always. He will see us through if we trust confidently in Him, rest quietly in Him, look stedfastly to Him, and walk obediently, in dependency upon Him.

Realize that the Lord Jesus is the Victor, and He enables us to be victorious. Apart from Him, we can do nothing.

How we so desperately need Him!

If you are full of weaknesses, rejoice! For you, therefore, have a great capacity for His strengths. Ask and allow God to perfect His strengths in you, in place of your weaknesses...

**In the following, final pages,**

let's seriously and earnestly consider the awesome time in which we live, spoken of by God's prophets of old and of today; a time of great darkness and of great light [Isaiah 60:1-2]; of great bondage and death while also being a time of great deliverance and life. We have come to the climax of this present age; the time for the demotion of man and the exaltation of the Son of God — the Lord Jesus: the one and only Christ...

Yes, *this* is the hour...

# "This Is The Hour"

*This is the hour* of conflict
And only what's of God will stand.
The forces of darkness will scatter
And all will fail that is of man.

*This is the hour* of fulfillment
Of all that the prophets have said.
And soon we will see a Body complete
With Jesus alone as its Head.

*This is the hour* of quickening
Our pace in pursuit of our quest
To know the Lord in His fullness
And always walk in His best.

For *this is the hour* of darkness
And *this is the hour* of light
And there shall be clear separation
Of that which is wrong and is right.

So choose the path of the Master
Who's called us to walk in His ways
And we shall be free and walk victoriously
As we obey all that He says.

Be done with pride and vainglory
And lay hold of Jesus our Life
For we will be blest if in Him we rest
And cease from all of our strife.

Lay aside chains of tradition
And all of the thinking of men.
To those who believe, they'll surely receive
Complete victory over all sin.

So saints of God, put on His armor
Of holiness, truth, and of light.
Lift up the sword — the word of the Lord —
And scatter the forces of night.

Come forth, you mighty warriors

Lift up the name of God's Son!
And the nations will hear and then they shall fear
In the knowledge of the Holy One.

Yes, saints arise in your places
And let God arise within
And darkness will flee and creation will see
The only Deliverer from sin.

For Jesus our Lord and our Captain
Stands armed, prepared for war
And His army He'll lead triumphantly
'til death has died and is no more.

Lift up your voice with jubilation
Declaring the praises of God
Who has called us to inherit glory
Through the righteousness of His Son.

Oh sing to the Lord a new song
Sing to the Lord all the earth
Sing to the Lord a new song
Tell of His unequaled worth!

Come worship the King of the ages
Yes worship the Lord God alone
And soon it shall be,
through His church fit and clean
God's Son's life will be made known.

***For this is the hour of Jesus***
When in power He shall be revealed
Yet, before every eye
sees Him break through the sky
He'll be seen in those who do His will.

"...the Lord, the Messiah,

Whom you seek, will *suddenly*

come to His temple..."

[Malachi 3:1b; based on AMP and NAS].


..."Yes, I am coming soon."

Amen. Come, Lord Jesus.

The grace of the Lord Jesus

be with God's people.

Amen.

[Revelation 22:20b-21; NIV].

Peace, strength, encouragement, and wisdom to all who desire to know God in His fullness and satisfy Him fully!

May you fulfill the highest calling of all, coming to intimately know and totally please the Lord Jesus Christ — the journey's Quest and Destination.

In Jesus' name,
*Larry Trammell*

# Acknowledgments

**Chris Strong:** A co-sharer in the joys and sufferings in the Kingdom; I respect and love you, brother.

**Cliff Custer:** Thank you for loving my family and me and for walking in such a precious spirit.

**Larry Davis:** Thanks for standing in faith for me, and for introducing me to Don. Larry was the first person I heard share about the Kingdom of God.

**Don Murphy ("Papa Don"):** Thank you for your example of "approachable spirituality," and for loving the Kingdom and its Lord. It was through Don that the Lord began to quicken to me that "the greater includes the lesser."

**Stephanie Ray Johnson:** Her labors of love in the realm of desktop publishing, as well as her warfare and precious encouragement have contributed immeasurably to the publication of this book. Thank you, my sister.

**Patti Greenblat:** Your frequent intercessions on my behalf are so very much appreciated.

**The Ghiotos (Vince, Jan, and the girls):** You were a family to me. Thank you.

**Lillian Schultz ("Hey You!"):** You were a mother to me, and I feel I owe you my life.

**Mom and Dad:** Thank you for exposing me to foundational Truth and for helping me to become established in "Music — art of the prophets. Among the gifts God has given, one of the most magnificent." Mom, thanks also for your great help in editing.

**Joe ("Dad") and Louise ("Mama") McBride:** My wonderful parents-in-law; my other set of parents.

**Cliff and Stacy:** The most wonderful and precious children in the universe!

**Alice:** My bride. My pride and joy. "Many daughters have done nobly, but you excel them all!" [Proverbs 31:29].

Thanks and peace to all the above and all you others out there who have added to and subtracted from (sometimes I've needed that too!) my life.

As you've done it to one of the least of His people, you've done it to Him.

You shall not lose your reward.

He and I both thank you.

# About The Author

Larry Trammell longs to see the Living God and His Son, the Lord Jesus Christ, revealed in the earth through the Church. Larry strongly stresses that this revealing of God and His kingdom will only occur as God's people keep their focus, pursuit, and love set on the Lord alone, and not on just the acquiring of things and knowledge from and about God, for "the greater includes the lesser."

With prophetic insight and unction, and with the psalmist's song, He has emphasized for years individual accountability and obedience to God. This he says must take place for God to form His people into a unified, effective instrument of worship and war in these last days.

Larry has traveled extensively with "The Sharrett Brothers," a musical and preaching ministry team. Now (and often with his wife; sometimes also with his children as well), he utilizes both the spoken word and music to declare the call and reality of the Kingdom of God. This occurs in teaching or preaching situations as well as in concerts and in the leading of others into worship of the Lord.

His vocation has included being a professional songwriter, vocalist, and keyboardist.

Residing near Atlanta, Georgia with his wife and children, he is available, as the Lord wills, to share the deposits God has worked and placed in him.

Your prayers on behalf of him and his family are *greatly* appreciated.

Larry may be reached and/or you can be placed on his mailing list by writing to:

**Larry Trammell**

**P. O. Box 956236**

**Duluth, GA 30136**

or you may call him at:

**(404) 476-0230**

Be looking for other fine publications as well as music from your friends at Ablaze Productions!, Inc.

Please feel free to contact us.

Ask for our materials by name at your favorite bookstore.

Peace to you in Jesus' name as you pursue Him.

We are:

**Ablaze Productions!, Inc.**

**6185 South Buford Highway**

**Suite C-155**

**Norcross, GA. 30071**

**(404) 416-0945**

P.S. — Of particular note is Larry Trammell's next book in the "READ AND TAKE HEED!" series, entitled "NUGGETS: A Gold Mine Of Proverbs And Wise, Practical Instruction." Many of the major points of "THE HIGHEST CALLING OF ALL" (as well as some additional points that are not covered) are contained in a concise format that reads very much like the book of Proverbs.

It will prove to be a tremendous aid for personal meditations and group discussions. Speakers and teachers will find it to be a ready and superb source for timely topics as well as for "power phrases" that will add impact to their presentations.

Let us know if we can assist you in getting a copy.

Also, quanity discounts are available on all of our products.